200 *Fast*
midweek meals

hamlyn | **all colour cookbook**

200 *Fast*
midweek meals

An Hachette UK Company
www.hachette.co.uk

First published in Great Britain in 2015 by
Hamlyn, an imprint of Octopus Publishing Group Ltd
Carmelite House
50 Victoria Embankment
London EC4Y 0DZ
www.octopusbooks.co.uk

Copyright © Octopus Publishing Group Ltd 2015

Recipes in this book have previously appeared in other
books published by Hamlyn.

ISBN 978 0 6006 2903 0

A CIP catalogue record for this book is available from the
British Library

Printed and bound in China

10 9 8 7 6 5 4 3 2

Standard level spoon measurements are used in all recipes.
1 tablespoon = one 15 ml spoon
1 teaspoon = one 5 ml spoon

Both imperial and metric measurements have been given
in all recipes. Use one set of measurements only and not a
mixture of both.

Eggs should be medium unless otherwise stated. The
Department of Health advises that eggs should not be
consumed raw. This book contains dishes made with raw or
lightly cooked eggs. It is prudent for more vulnerable people
such as pregnant and nursing mothers, invalids, the elderly,
babies and young children to avoid uncooked or lightly
cooked dishes made with eggs. Once prepared, these dishes
should be kept refrigerated and used promptly.

Milk should be full fat unless otherwise stated.

Fresh herbs should be used unless otherwise stated.
If unavailable, use dried herbs as an alternative but
halve the quantities stated.

Ovens should be preheated to the specific temperature – if
using a fan-assisted oven, follow manufacturer's instructions
for adjusting the time and the temperature.

contents

introduction

This book offers a new and flexible approach to meal planning for busy cooks and lets you choose the recipe option that best fits the time you have available. Inside you will find 200 dishes that will inspire you and motivate you to get cooking every day of the year.

All the recipes take a maximum of 30 minutes to cook. Some take as little as 20 minutes and, amazingly, many take only 10 minutes.

On every page you'll find a main recipe plus a short-cut version or a fancier variation if you have a bit more time to spare. Whatever you go for, you'll find a huge range of super-quick recipes to get you through the week.

midweek meals

For many, cooking in the week is a bore; it is a 'must-do' activity rather than a 'like-to' activity. Energy and creativity levels are low, there's very little time and there are other things you need to be getting on with. So we have come up with this book to put the pleasure back into cooking meals midweek.

The key to midweek meal success is preparation. Use part of your lunch hour or some time at the weekend to browse through this book and choose four or five meals that you'd like to serve in the week. Then, once you've worked out what ingredients you need, ensure you get everything in stock ready for the beginning of the week. Don't forget internet shopping and home-delivery services – they are designed for busy people and can be arranged for times that suit you and your busy schedule.

mix it up

• Eat fish at least twice a week, as it helps to reduce the risk of heart disease, is rich in B and D vitamins and contains high levels of omega-3 fatty acids, which are great for heart health.
• Chicken can be eaten as often as your budget allows, but buy organic where possible.
• If you are a red meat addict, choose lean cuts where possible and those that lend

themselves to quick cooking. Limit eating red meat to twice a week.

• Offal is an excellent source of vitamins, copper, iron and zinc; however, as the liver tends to accumulate chemical residues from the animal, limit your intake to once a week.

• Nuts and seeds are nutritional gems. They are low in saturated fats, high in protein and fibre and are brimming with B vitamins and many useful minerals.

• Eggs are a quick and healthy protein source, and low in saturated fat – current thinking is that up to six eggs a week is a perfectly healthy addition to your diet.

• Mix up your vegetables as much as your budget allows. Include root and leafy veg and as many different colours as you can. All

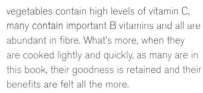

vegetables contain high levels of vitamin C, many contain important B vitamins and all are abundant in fibre. What's more, when they are cooked lightly and quickly, as many are in this book, their goodness is retained and their benefits are felt all the more.

• Always choose whole grains because these are good for your heart and also keep you feeling fuller for longer.

the storecupboard

To whizz up a magical meal in minutes, you are going to need some basics in your cupboards. These include plain flour, cornflour and a bottle of UHT milk for making emergency sauces, cans of chopped tomatoes, chickpeas and beans, passata, tomato purée, strong English mustard and a good selection of oils including a basic vegetable oil such as sunflower oil, a good-quality olive oil, and some more alternative flavours, such as peanut, sesame and walnut. Always have a decent balsamic vinegar in the cupboard, and, for those dishes with an oriental twist, stock up on coconut milk, soy sauce, fish sauce, sweet chilli dipping sauce and hoi sin, plus a selection of your preferred noodles and rice.

Don't be afraid to buy some 'cheat' ingredients for those super-quick meals you're going to prepare: pesto sauces, ready-made pizza bases and Thai curry paste are must-haves for busy days, and don't forget that you can buy garlic, fresh root ginger and lemon grass

in paste form, which can be quickly and easily squeezed into the pan when cooking.

Jars of preserved vegetables are a tasty, easy addition to many pastas, salads and rice dishes, and can be stored for months (if not years) very successfully as long as they are kept cool. Therefore, it would not go amiss to treat yourself to some jars of artichoke hearts, olives and roasted red peppers, and, to add the occasional kick to your cooking, keep some capers and anchovies in stock, too; you'd be surprised how much these tiny additions bring to a meal.

You may not think of yourself as a gardener, but learning to keep a few potted herbs on the windowsill will benefit you no end when it comes to adding quick and easy flavour to a midweek meal. Easy-maintenance herbs include basil, coriander, chives and rosemary. Oregano and thyme can be a little trickier to keep; however, these can be bought fresh in bunches and frozen for when you need them. Don't be concerned if the leaves go very dark or black – they will retain their flavour.

the refrigerator and freezer

Make space in your refrigerator for some of the key ingredients that form the basis of many meals: onions, garlic, hard cheese such as Cheddar and a good strong Parmesan, crème fraîche and some natural yogurt. Keep quartered lemons and limes, fresh root ginger and chillies in the freezer, plus nutrient-rich vegetables that freeze well, such as spinach, peas or sweetcorn kernels. Separate and freeze bacon, chicken and fish fillets and sausages in small servings ready for easy defrosting; or buy bags of frozen prawns, mussels or mixed seafood for an easy addition to soups, stews and stir-fries.

Remember, too, that bread freezes well; bags of muffins and burger buns kept in the freezer are sure to get good use. When a loaf of bread is no longer fresh enough to eat in slices, whizz up the loaf in a food processor and freeze the breadcrumbs in small food bags ready for coating chicken or fish fillets.

poultry

parmesan chicken escalopes

Serves **4**

Total cooking time **20 minutes**

2 **skinless chicken breast fillets**, halved horizontally
2 tablespoons **plain flour**
1 **egg**, beaten
125 g (4 oz) **fresh ciabatta breadcrumbs**
75 g (3 oz) **Parmesan cheese**, grated
3 tablespoons **sunflower oil**
4 **small baguettes**, halved lengthways
4 tablespoons **mayonnaise**
4 small handfuls of **mixed salad leaves**
salt and **pepper**

Place the chicken halves between 2 pieces of clingfilm and beat with a rolling pin to flatten slightly. Put the flour on a plate and the egg in a dish. On a separate plate, mix together the breadcrumbs and Parmesan and season with salt and pepper.

Lightly coat each piece of chicken in flour, shaking off any excess, dip into the beaten egg and coat in the breadcrumb mixture, pressing it on firmly.

Heat the oil in a large frying pan, add the chicken and cook for about 5 minutes, turning once, until golden, crisp and cooked through.

Fill the baguette pieces with mayonnaise, salad leaves and the hot chicken.

For chicken Caesar baguette, heat 2 tablespoons sunflower oil in a wok or large frying pan and stir-fry 2 skinless chicken breast fillets, cut into strips, for about 5 minutes or until cooked through. Pile into pieces of baguette with mixed salad leaves and a drizzle of Caesar salad dressing. **Total cooking time 10 minutes.**

turkey, lemon & chilli stew

Serves **4**

Total cooking time **30 minutes**

875 g (1¾ lb) **turkey breast steaks**, cut into bite-sized pieces

2 tablespoons **sunflower oil**

4 **garlic cloves**, crushed

1 **onion**, finely chopped

2 teaspoons **dried chilli flakes**

10–12 **baby onions**, peeled

2 **carrots**, peeled and cut into bite-sized pieces

2 **potatoes**, peeled and cut into bite-sized pieces

1 tablespoon **sweet smoked paprika**

3 tablespoons **lemon juice**

6 tablespoons finely chopped **flat leaf parsley**

500 ml (17 fl oz) hot **chicken stock**

salt and **pepper**

crusty bread, to serve

Put the turkey in a bowl and season well. Heat the oil in a large frying pan, add the turkey and cook over a high heat, stirring occasionally, for 2–3 minutes or until browned all over.

Transfer to a heavy-based saucepan, stir in the remaining ingredients and bring to the boil. Reduce the heat to medium and cook, uncovered, for 20 minutes or until the turkey is cooked through and the vegetables are tender.

Ladle into warmed bowls and serve with crusty bread.

For quick turkey, chilli & lemon rice, heat 2 tablespoons sunflower oil in a large frying pan until hot, add 4 chopped garlic cloves, 1 deseeded and chopped red chilli and ½ small chopped onion. Stir-fry for 1–2 minutes. Add 500 g (1 lb) ready-cooked rice, 1 tablespoon sweet smoked paprika and 400 g (13 oz) diced ready-cooked turkey breast and stir-fry for a further 3–4 minutes until piping hot. Remove from the heat, season and stir in the grated rind of ½ lemon and 4 tablespoons chopped flat leaf parsley. **Total cooking time 10 minutes.**

thai chicken soup

Serves **4**
Total cooking time **10 minutes**

2 x 400 g (13 oz) cans
  reduced-fat coconut milk
125 ml (4 fl oz) hot **chicken
  stock**
1 tablespoon **Thai red curry
  paste**
2 **skinless chicken breast
  fillets**, very thinly sliced
200 g (7 oz) **mangetout**
200 g (7 oz) **bean sprouts**

Place the coconut milk, stock and curry paste in a large saucepan and bring to the boil.

Add the chicken and cook for 2 minutes, then add the mangetout and bean sprouts and cook for a further 5 minutes until the chicken is cooked through.

Serve ladled into warmed serving bowls.

For Thai green curry stir-fry, heat 2 tablespoons vegetable oil in a large wok or heavy-based frying pan and cook 1 roughly chopped lemon grass stalk, 1 cm (½ inch) piece of fresh root ginger, peeled and roughly chopped, and 4 thinly sliced skinless chicken breast fillets over a medium-high heat, stirring frequently, for 5 minutes until browned and cooked through. Add 200 g (7 oz) mangetout, 1 cored, deseeded and roughly chopped red pepper and 200 g (7 oz) bean sprouts and stir-fry over a high heat for 2–3 minutes. Blend 1 tablespoon Thai green curry paste with 6 tablespoons coconut milk, then pour over the stir-fry and cook, tossing, for a further 2 minutes. **Total cooking time 20 minutes.**

potato, chicken & bacon gratin

Serves **4**
Total cooking time **30 minutes**

500 g (1 lb) **potatoes**,
  scrubbed but not peeled
  and thinly sliced
2 tablespoons **olive oil**
1 **onion**, thinly sliced
2 **chicken breast fillets**, thinly
  sliced
6 **back bacon rashers**, thinly
  sliced
3 tablespoons **thyme leaves**,
  plus extra sprigs, to garnish
  (optional)
300 ml (½ pint) **double cream**
5 tablespoons grated
  Parmesan cheese
salt and **pepper**

Cook the potatoes in a large saucepan of lightly salted boiling water for 10 minutes until just tender, then drain.

Meanwhile, heat the oil in a large, heavy-based frying pan and cook the onion, chicken and bacon over a high heat, stirring occasionally, for 5 minutes or until the chicken is cooked through.

Layer the potatoes in a large, shallow gratin dish with the chicken, bacon, onion and a scattering of thyme leaves, ending with a layer of potatoes. Season the cream with a little salt and pepper and pour over the potatoes. Scatter over the Parmesan and cook under a preheated hot grill for 4–5 minutes until the topping is golden and the cream bubbling. Garnish with thyme sprigs, if liked.

For chicken, bacon & thyme stir-fry, heat 2 tablespoons olive oil in a large, heavy-based frying pan and cook 3 thinly sliced chicken breast fillets and 175 g (6 oz) chopped back bacon pieces for 8 minutes, stirring occasionally, then add 1 tablespoon thyme leaves and 400 ml (14 fl oz) crème fraîche. Season generously and serve with instant mashed potato, with grated Parmesan cheese sprinkled over. **Total cooking time 15 minutes.**

smoky barbecue chicken pizza

Serves **4**

Total cooking time **30 minutes**

250 g (8 oz) **plain flour**

½ teaspoon **salt**

1 teaspoon **bicarbonate of soda**

pinch of **sugar**

25 g (1 oz) cold **butter**

150 ml (¼ pint) **buttermilk** or **natural yogurt**

4 tablespoons **ready-made tomato pizza sauce**

250 g (8 oz) **ready-cooked chicken**, chopped

2 tablespoons **smoky barbecue sauce**

125 g (4 oz) **roasted peppers from a jar**, drained and chopped

150 g (5 oz) **mozzarella cheese**, sliced

Sift the flour into a bowl with the salt, bicarbonate of soda and sugar. Coarsely grate the butter into the mixture. Stir well to break up any clumps of butter, add the buttermilk or yogurt and mix to a soft dough.

Knead the dough lightly until smooth, shape into a ball and pat out with your hands to a large circle about 30 cm (12 inches) across. Place on a baking sheet.

Spread the tomato sauce over the dough, leaving a small border around the edge. Mix together the chicken and barbecue sauce and spread over the pizza. Arrange the peppers and mozzarella on top and bake in a preheated oven, 200°C (400°F), Gas Mark 6, for 15 minutes until the base is cooked and the topping is golden.

For thin & crispy barbecue pizza, unroll a ready-rolled sheet of shortcrust pastry and place on a baking sheet. Spread 4 tablespoons ready-made tomato pizza sauce over the top. Chop 250 g (8 oz) ready-cooked chicken, mix with 2 tablespoons smoky barbecue sauce and scatter over the top. Chop 125 g (4 oz) roasted red peppers from a jar, slice 150 g (5 oz) mozzarella cheese and arrange on top. Bake in a preheated oven, 200°C (400°F), Gas Mark 6, for 15 minutes or until crisp and golden. **Total cooking time 20 minutes.**

piri-piri spiced turkey fillets

Serves **4**

Total cooking time **30 minutes**

450 g (14½ oz) **turkey breast fillets**, cut into strips
400 g (13 oz) can **chickpeas**, drained
1 tablespoon **lime juice**
5–6 tablespoons **soured cream**
4 **multiseed tortillas**, warmed
lime wedges
salt and **pepper**

Piri-piri marinade
2 tablespoons **sun-dried tomato paste**
1 teaspoon **oregano**
2 tablespoons **red wine vinegar**
1 teaspoon **hot smoked paprika**
2 **garlic cloves**, finely chopped
2 **long red chillies**, finely chopped (deseed for less heat)

Place the tomato paste, oregano, red wine vinegar, paprika, garlic and chillies for the piri-piri marinade in a mini chopper or the bowl of a small food processor. Season generously with salt and pepper, then process until smooth.

Tip the turkey strips into a bowl and scrape over the piri-piri marinade, reserving 1 tablespoon to make the hummus. Mix all the ingredients until the turkey is well coated in the marinade, cover and set aside to marinate for about 10 minutes.

Meanwhile, place the chickpeas, lime juice and reserved piri-piri marinade in a food processor or blender and pulse briefly, adding enough soured cream to give a smooth, creamy consistency.

Arrange the marinated turkey strips on a foil-lined baking sheet and slide under a preheated hot grill for 5–7 minutes, turning frequently, until cooked through and lightly charred.

Serve the grilled turkey fillets with the hummus, warmed tortillas and lime wedges on the side.

For quick piri-piri turkey steaks with hummus, place 4 turkey breast steaks between 2 sheets of clingfilm and batter with a rolling pin to flatten. Coat the turkey steaks with 4 tablespoons ready-made piri-piri sauce, then place on a foil-lined baking sheet and slide under a preheated hot grill for 5–7 minutes until cooked, turning once. Stir 2 teaspoons of the ready-made piri-piri sauce into 300 g (10 oz) reduced-fat hummus. Serve the turkey steaks with the hummus, warmed tortillas and lime wedges. **Total cooking time 20 minutes.**

griddled chicken & fruity couscous

Serves **4**

Total cooking time **30 minutes**

4 **boneless, skinless chicken breasts**, about 150 g (5 oz) each

6 tablespoons **balsamic vinegar**

350 ml (12 fl oz) boiled **water**, slightly cooled

175 g (6 oz) **couscous**

3 tablespoons **olive oil**

1 **avocado**, stoned, peeled and roughly chopped

1 large **tomato**, roughly chopped

5 tablespoons chopped **fresh coriander**

50 g (2 oz) **raisins**

4 tablespoons **pumpkin seeds**

salt

Place the chicken in a non-metallic container, pour over the vinegar and turn to coat. Cover and leave to marinate for 5 minutes.

Pour the measurement water over the couscous in a bowl and season with a little salt. Cover and leave to absorb the water for 10 minutes.

Meanwhile, heat 1 tablespoon of the oil in a large griddle or frying pan and cook the chicken over a medium heat, turning once, for 10–12 minutes until browned and cooked through; when the chicken is pierced, the juices should run clear.

Make the salsa while the chicken is cooking by mixing together in a bowl the avocado, tomato, 1 tablespoon of the remaining oil and 1 tablespoon of the coriander.

Stir the remaining oil into the couscous, then add the raisins, pumpkin seeds and remaining coriander and toss again. Serve on warmed serving plates topped with the chicken, with the salsa spooned over.

For sun-dried tomato & chicken couscous, cook a 110 g (3¾ oz) pack tomato and onion couscous according to the pack instructions. Meanwhile, heat 3 tablespoons oil from a 185 g (6½ oz) tub sun-dried tomatoes in oil in a large saucepan and heat through 400 g (13 oz) ready-cooked chicken breast chunks for 3 minutes. Add 5 chopped sun-dried tomatoes and 1 red pepper, cored, deseeded and diced, and cook over a medium heat, stirring, for 5 minutes. Stir in 2 chopped spring onions, 1 tablespoon each clear honey and balsamic vinegar, 1 teaspoon wholegrain mustard and the couscous. **Total cooking time 15 minutes.**

mozzarella chicken melts

Serves **4**

Total cooking time **20 minutes**

1 tablespoon **ready-made sun-dried tomato pesto**

2 tablespoons **olive oil**

2 **chicken breast fillets**, halved horizontally

4 thick slices of **sourdough bread**

2 tablespoons **ready-made tapenade**

175 g (6 oz) **cherry tomatoes**, halved

small handful of **basil leaves**, roughly torn

150 g (5 oz) **mozzarella cheese**, sliced

green salad, to serve

Mix together the pesto and 1 tablespoon of the oil and spread over both sides of the chicken pieces.

Heat the remaining olive oil in a frying pan, add the chicken and cook for 8–10 minutes, turning once, until the chicken is cooked through.

Toast both sides of the sourdough bread. Spread one side with the tapenade, then top with the cooked chicken, tomatoes, basil and mozzarella. Cook under a preheated hot grill until the tomatoes are hot and the mozzarella has melted. Serve with a simple green salad.

For Italian chicken toasties, butter 8 slices of crusty bread. Spread the unbuttered side of 4 slices with 2 tablespoons ready-made tapenade. Top with 200 g (7 oz) sliced ready-cooked chicken, 2 sliced tomatoes, a handful of basil leaves and 150 g (5 oz) sliced mozzarella cheese. Top with the remaining bread, butter side up. Cook in a sandwich toaster for about 5 minutes until golden and crisp or in a frying pan, turning once, until the bread is crisp and the filling is hot. **Total cooking time 10 minutes.**

chicken, leek & tarragon pie

Serves **4**

Total cooking time **30 minutes**

2 **leeks**, cleaned, trimmed and
    cut into thin rounds
8 **ready-cooked chicken legs**,
    bones removed and meat
    roughly chopped
125 g (4 oz) thick piece of
    cooked ham, cubed
150 ml (¼ pint) **crème fraîche**
handful of **tarragon leaves**,
    chopped
375 g (12 oz) **ready-rolled
    shortcrust pastry**
1 **egg**, lightly beaten
salt and **pepper**

To serve
peas
mashed potatoes

Put the leeks in a sieve or colander and pour over a kettleful of boiling water until starting to wilt. Mix the leeks with the chicken meat, ham, crème fraîche and tarragon and season. Transfer the mixture to a 23 cm (9 inch) pie dish.

Place the pastry on top, crimp around the edges and cut away any excess pastry. Make a small slit in the centre of the pastry and brush all over with the egg. Cook in a preheated oven, 220°C (425°F), Gas Mark 7, for 20–25 minutes until golden and bubbling. Serve with peas and mashed potatoes.

For chicken, tarragon & bacon salad, cook 4 streaky bacon rashers under a preheated hot grill for 7 minutes, turning once, until crisp. Meanwhile, mix together 200 ml (7 fl oz) natural yogurt, 4 tablespoons mayonnaise, 1 tablespoon wholegrain mustard and a handful of chopped tarragon leaves and season to taste. Combine with 3 sliced ready-cooked chicken breasts. Toss the leaves from 1 lettuce and 1 head of chicory with 3 tablespoons olive oil and 1 tablespoon white wine vinegar. Arrange on a plate with 75 g (3 oz) sliced radishes. Top with the chicken and crumble over the bacon to serve. **Total cooking time 10 minutes.**

saffron roasted chicken

Serves **4**

Total cooking time **20 minutes**

3 tablespoons **milk**

pinch of **saffron threads**

75 ml (3 fl oz) **natural yogurt**

2 **garlic cloves**, crushed

2 teaspoons peeled and finely grated **fresh root ginger**

25 g (1 oz) **ground almonds**

2 teaspoons toasted **cumin seeds**

4 **boneless, skinless chicken breasts**, about 150 g (5 oz) each

15 g (½ oz) **butter**, plus extra for greasing

25 g (1 oz) **flaked almonds**

handful of **mint leaves**, finely sliced

1 **green chilli**, deseeded and chopped

salt and **pepper**

To serve

tomato salad

boiled **rice**

Heat the milk, add the saffron and set aside.

Mix together the yogurt, garlic, ginger, ground almonds and cumin seeds and season well. Coat the chicken in the mixture, place on a lightly greased baking sheet and cook in a preheated oven, 220°C (425°F), Gas Mark 7, for 10 minutes.

Pour over the saffron liquid, dot with the butter and scatter over the flaked almonds, then cook for 5 minutes more or until the chicken is cooked through; when the chicken is pierced, the juices should run clear.

Sprinkle over the mint and chilli and serve with a tomato salad and boiled rice.

For chicken chapatti wraps, mix 300 g (10 oz) chicken stir-fry strips with 25 g (1 oz) natural yogurt, a pinch of saffron threads, 1 teaspoon ground cumin and a pinch of dried chilli flakes. Season to taste and drizzle over 1 tablespoon vegetable oil. Heat a griddle pan until smoking and cook the chicken for 3–4 minutes on each side until cooked through. Place on 4 warmed chapattis and top with chopped tomatoes, sliced Little Gem lettuce leaves and some chopped fresh coriander. **Total cooking time 10 minutes.**

spicy stir-fried chilli chicken

Serves **4**

Total cooking time **20 minutes**

400 g (13 oz) **skinless
    chicken breast fillets**, sliced

3 tablespoons **light soy sauce**

3 tablespoons **rice wine**

1 tablespoon **cornflour**

3 tablespoons **vegetable oil**

75 g (3 oz) **cashew nuts**

2 **spring onions**, sliced

3 **garlic cloves**, sliced

1 tablespoon peeled and
    grated **fresh root ginger**

1 teaspoon **chilli sauce**

2 teaspoons **caster sugar**

3–4 tablespoons **water**

To serve

boiled **rice**

wilted **watercress**

Mix the chicken with 1 tablespoon each of the soy sauce and rice wine and 1 teaspoon of the cornflour. Leave to marinate for 5–10 minutes.

Heat 1 tablespoon of the oil in a wok or large frying pan, add the cashew nuts and stir around the pan for 2 minutes until lightly browned, then remove from the pan. Heat the remaining oil and cook the chicken for 5–7 minutes until just cooked through. Remove from the pan.

Add the spring onions, garlic and ginger and cook for 30 seconds, then return the chicken and nuts to the pan. Stir in the remaining soy sauce, rice wine and cornflour, the chilli sauce, caster sugar and measurement water. Heat until bubbling and slightly thickened. Serve with boiled rice and wilted watercress.

For chilli chicken skewers, cut 2 large skinless chicken breast fillets into long thin strips and thread on to metal skewers. Mix together 1 tablespoon each chilli sauce and vegetable oil with 2 tablespoons light soy sauce and rub over the chicken. Heat a griddle pan until smoking and cook the skewers for 3–4 minutes on each side until just cooked through. Serve with ready-cooked rice noodles tossed together with 2 tablespoons each soy sauce and rice wine and ¼ cucumber, thinly sliced. **Total cooking time 10 minutes.**

smoked duck & orange salad

Serves **4**

Total cooking time **10 minutes**

2 large **oranges**

1 tablespoon **rice wine vinegar**

3 tablespoons **vegetable oil**

150 g (5 oz) **watercress**

1 head of **chicory**, leaves separated

1 **spring onion**, sliced

150 g (5 oz) **radishes**, sliced

250 g (8 oz) **sliced smoked duck breast**

salt and **pepper**

Cut the peel from the oranges using a sharp knife. Divide the oranges into segments by cutting between the membranes, holding them over a bowl to catch the juice. Mix the orange juice with the vinegar and oil and season well.

Toss the dressing with the watercress, chicory leaves and spring onion. Arrange the salad on serving plates with the orange segments, radishes and smoked duck.

For smoked duck risotto with watercress, heat 25 g (1 oz) butter and 1 tablespoon olive oil in a saucepan. Add 1 finely chopped shallot and cook for 5 minutes until softened. Stir in 300 g (10 oz) risotto rice and 1 teaspoon finely grated orange rind, then add 125 ml (4 fl oz) dry white wine. Cook until bubbled away, then gradually stir in 900 ml (1½ pints) hot chicken stock, a little at a time, stirring frequently, allowing the rice to absorb the stock before adding more. When the rice is soft, after about 15 minutes, add 100 g (3½ oz) frozen peas and 125 g (4 oz) chopped watercress. Cook until wilted, then add 50 g (2 oz) grated Parmesan cheese and season to taste. Top with 150 g (5 oz) sliced smoked duck breast to serve. **Total cooking time 30 minutes.**

lemon chicken with wilted greens

Serves **4**

Total cooking time **30 minutes**

8 **boneless chicken thighs**
4 tablespoons **thyme leaves**
1 tablespoon **olive oil**
finely grated rind and juice of
   1 **lemon**
1 tablespoon **Dijon mustard**
2 x 200 ml (7 fl oz) cartons
   crème fraîche
200 g (7 oz) **baby spinach
   leaves**
pepper
creamy mashed potato or
   cooked rice, to serve

Season the chicken thighs with plenty of pepper and roll in the thyme leaves. Heat the oil in a large, heavy-based frying pan and cook the chicken thighs over a medium heat for 20 minutes, turning frequently for the first 10 minutes, then covering with a lid for the final 10 minutes, until cooked through; when the chicken is pierced, the juices should run clear.

Add the lemon rind and juice to the pan and toss with the chicken. Mix the mustard into one of the cartons of crème fraîche and then add both cartons of crème fraiche to the pan with the spinach leaves. Toss and heat for 2–3 minutes until the spinach has wilted and the sauce is hot.

Serve with creamy mashed potato or rice.

For watercress chicken with capers, garlic & lemon, roughly chop 85 g (3 ¼ oz) watercress, ½ garlic clove and 1 tablespoon capers. Mix with the finely grated rind of 1 lemon and season with salt and pepper. Place on a plate and roll 350 g (11 ½ oz) chicken mini-breast fillets in the watercress mixture until each is evenly coated. Heat ½ tablespoon olive oil in a large frying pan, add the chicken and any remaining watercress mixture and cook over a medium heat for 3–4 minutes on each side until cooked through. Serve with a couscous salad. **Total cooking time 10 minutes.**

turkey burgers with spicy salsa

Serves **4**
Total cooking time **20 minutes**

500 g (1 lb) **lean minced turkey**
finely grated rind of **1 lime**
3 **spring onions**, finely chopped
1 tablespoon **sweet soy sauce** or **ketjap manis**
1 teaspoon **ground cumin**
100 g (3½ oz) **fresh breadcrumbs**
1 small **egg**, lightly beaten
4 small **ciabatta-style buns**
2 **Cos lettuce hearts**, shredded, to serve

Spicy salsa
250 g (8 oz) **cherry tomatoes**, quartered
1 **red chilli**, deseeded and finely chopped
2 **spring onions**, finely sliced
1 tablespoon **lime juice**
1 tablespoon **sweet soy sauce** or **ketjap manis**
1 small bunch of **fresh coriander**, chopped
1 **firm, ripe avocado**, stoned, peeled and diced

Place the minced turkey in a large bowl with the lime rind, spring onions, soy sauce or ketjap manis, cumin, breadcrumbs and egg. Mix until well combined, then using your hands, form into 8 flattened patties.

Transfer the burgers to a grill rack and slide under a preheated medium-hot grill for 3–4 minutes each side or until browned and cooked through.

Meanwhile, make the spicy salsa by putting all the salsa ingredients in a bowl and stirring until well combined. Set aside.

Cut the ciabatta rolls in half and place the rolls, cut side up, on the grill rack alongside the burgers. Toast for 1–2 minutes until lightly charred.

Place the cooked burgers on the toasted rolls with the lettuce leaves and top with the salsa. Serve as open burgers.

For healthy turkey & salsa Granary baguettes, make the spicy salsa as above. Cut 4 small Granary baguettes in half lengthways and fill each baguette with one-quarter of a 75 g (3 oz) bag of mixed leaves, 1 thick slice of ready-cooked, hand-carved roast turkey and 1–2 spoonfuls of the salsa, then serve. **Total cooking time 10 minutes.**

crispy salt & pepper chicken

Serves **4**

Total cooking time **30 minutes**

8 **chicken thighs**
50 g (2 oz) **plain flour**
½ teaspoon **salt flakes**
1 teaspoon **ground black pepper**
1 tablespoon **olive oil**
3 teaspoons **thyme leaves**, to garnish
green vegetables or **crisp salad**, to serve (optional)

Tighten the flesh and skin around the bone of each chicken thigh and pierce with a cocktail stick so that the skin remains taut.

Put the flour in a large bowl with half the salt and pepper and toss the thighs in the seasoned flour until lightly coated.

Heat the oil in a large, heavy-based frying pan and cook the chicken, skin side up, for 5 minutes, turning once, until golden.

Transfer the chicken to a roasting tin, skin side up, and scatter over the remaining salt and pepper. Cook in a preheated oven, 200°C (400°F), Gas Mark 6, for 20–25 minutes until the chicken is golden and cooked through; when the chicken is pierced, the juices should run clear.

Scatter over the thyme leaves to garnish and serve with simple green vegetables or a crisp salad, if liked.

For salt & pepper chicken mini-fillets, put 50 g (2 oz) plain flour in a bowl and season with 1 teaspoon ground black pepper and a little salt. Toss 500 g (1 lb) chicken mini-fillets in the seasoned flour until lightly coated. Heat 4 tablespoons olive oil in a large, heavy-based frying pan or wok and cook the chicken over a high heat for 7–8 minutes until golden, crisp in places and cooked through. Remove from the pan with a slotted spoon and drain on kitchen paper before serving hot with mustard mayonnaise and a salad, if liked. **Total cooking time 10 minutes.**

chicken, chorizo & sage skewers

Serves **4**

Total cooking time **20 minutes**

4 **skinless chicken thighs**,
  each cut into 4 pieces
4 small **cooking chorizo**,
  halved
12 **sage leaves**
1 tablespoon **olive oil**
2 teaspoons **wholegrain
  mustard**

To serve
baby spinach leaves
crusty bread

Thread the chicken, chorizo and sage leaves on to 4 metal skewers. Mix together the olive oil and wholegrain mustard and brush over the skewers.

Cook on a hot griddle pan or under a preheated hot grill for 10–15 minutes, turning occasionally and brushing with more of the mustard mixture, until the chicken and chorizo are cooked.

Slide the chicken and chorizo off the skewers and serve with baby spinach leaves and crusty bread.

For chicken & chorizo pasta, cook 375 g (12 oz) quick-cook pasta shapes in a saucepan of lightly salted boiling water for 5–8 minutes or until tender. Meanwhile, fry 75 g (3 oz) sliced cured chorizo in a dry frying pan for 2 minutes. Add 350 g (11½ oz) ready-made tomato pasta sauce and 175 g (6 oz) chopped ready-cooked chicken. Heat through, drain the pasta and add to the sauce. Mix well and serve with grated Parmesan cheese. **Total cooking time 10 minutes.**

cheesy turkey & gnocchi bake

Serves **4**

Total cooking time **25 minutes**

750 g (1½ lb) **fresh gnocchi**

200 g (7 oz) **quark cheese** or **extra-light cream cheese**

125 g (4 oz) **strong blue cheese**, such as Gorgonzola Piccante or Stilton, crumbled

2 tablespoons snipped **chives**

200 g (7 oz) **ready-cooked smoked turkey**, cut into strips

200 g (7 oz) **frozen chopped spinach**, defrosted

2 **spring onions**, thinly sliced

salt and **black pepper**

To serve (optional)
green leaf salad
crusty bread

Bring a large saucepan of lightly salted water to the boil and cook the gnocchi for 2 minutes until cooked through, or according to the pack instructions. Drain well, then tip back into the saucepan.

Meanwhile, gently warm the quark or cream cheese, blue cheese and chives in a frying pan, then season well with pepper.

Remove from the heat, stir in the smoked turkey and spinach and gently fold the sauce into the cooked gnocchi.

Scrape the gnocchi and sauce into an ovenproof dish, scatter with the spring onions and place in a preheated oven 220°C (425°F), Gas Mark 7, for 15–18 minutes until golden and bubbling.

Serve the baked gnocchi with a crisp green leaf salad and crusty bread, if liked.

For baby gnocchi with creamy blue cheese & turkey sauce, cook 750 g (1½ lb) fresh tricolour baby gnocchi as above. Drain and spoon into warmed deep bowls. Meanwhile, melt 125 g (4 oz) Gorgonzola Piccante with 275 ml (9 fl oz) low-fat single cream in a frying pan over a low heat, stirring. Stir in 2 tablespoons snipped chives and season with pepper. Simmer for 1–2 minutes, take off the heat and stir in 200 g (7 oz) ready-cooked smoked turkey, cut into strips. Pour the sauce over the gnocchi and serve with sliced spring onions. **Total cooking time 10 minutes.**

oriental chicken satay stir-fry

Serves **2**

Total cooking time **20 minutes**

2 tablespoons **sesame oil**

300 g (10 oz) **skinless chicken breast fillets**, cut into long, thick strips

1 bunch of large **spring onions**, halved lengthways

1 **orange pepper**, cored, deseeded and cut into thick strips

1 head of **pak choi**, about 175 g (6 oz), leaves separated

boiled **rice**, to serve (optional)

Satay sauce

150 ml (¼ pint) boiling **water**

4 tablespoons **smooth peanut butter**

2 tablespoons **soy sauce**

1 tablespoon **sweet chilli sauce**

Heat the oil in a large wok or frying pan, add the chicken strips and stir-fry over a high heat for 5 minutes until golden in places. Add the spring onions and stir-fry for a further 3 minutes.

Add the orange pepper and continue to stir-fry for 3 minutes until the chicken and vegetables are cooked through. Add the pak choi and cook for 1 minute. Remove from the heat.

Place the sauce, place the measurement water for the sauce in a small saucepan with the remaining ingredients and bring to the boil, stirring with a balloon whisk until smooth. Pour into the wok with the chicken and vegetables and toss to coat. Serve immediately with rice, if liked.

For quick chicken satay stir-fry, heat 1 tablespoon sesame oil in a wok, add 250 g (8 oz) chicken mini-fillets and stir-fry over a high heat for 5 minutes until golden. Add a 300 g (10 oz) pack ready-prepared stir-fry vegetables and 4 spring onions, roughly chopped, and stir-fry for a further 2–3 minutes until tender. In a jug, mix together 1 tablespoon soy sauce, 2 tablespoons smooth peanut butter and 4 tablespoons boiling water. Pour into the wok and toss and cook for a further 1 minute. Serve hot. **Total cooking time 10 minutes.**

speedy stuffed roast chicken

Serves **4**

Total cooking time **30 minutes**

4 **boneless, skinless chicken breasts**, about 125 g (4 oz) each
50 g (2 oz) **sage and onion stuffing mix**
4 **bacon rashers**
250 g (8 oz) **baby carrots**
3 tablespoons **olive oil**
2 tablespoons chopped **parsley**

Lay the chicken breasts on a board and slice them lengthways almost all the way through, leaving a 'hinge' at one long end.

Make up the stuffing mix according to the pack instructions and use 1 tablespoon of the stuffing to fill each of the breasts. Wrap each tightly with a bacon rasher to keep the stuffing in place.

Put the chicken and carrots in 1 or 2 roasting tins, drizzle over the oil and shake gently to coat in the oil. Roast in a preheated oven, 200°C (400°F), Gas Mark 6, for 25 minutes or until the chicken is golden and cooked through; when the chicken is pierced, the juices should run clear. Scatter over the parsley to garnish before serving.

For simple chicken & bacon pan-fry with sage & onion, heat 3 tablespoons olive oil in a large, heavy-based frying pan and cook 1 roughly sliced red onion, 375 g (12 oz) chicken mini-fillets and 4 roughly chopped back bacon rashers over a high heat, stirring occasionally, for 8–10 minutes or until golden and soft. Add 1 tablespoon chopped sage leaves and cook for a few more seconds before serving with instant mashed potatoes and chicken gravy, if liked. **Total cooking time 15 minutes.**

simple chicken korma

Serves **4**

Total cooking time **20 minutes**

2 tablespoons **vegetable oil**

1 large **onion**, roughly chopped

500 g (1 lb) **skinless chicken breast fillets**, diced

1 teaspoon peeled and finely chopped **fresh root ginger**

1 teaspoon finely chopped **garlic**

1 teaspoon **dried chilli flakes**

1 tablespoon **ground coriander**

1 teaspoon **ground turmeric**

1 teaspoon **garam masala**

4 tablespoons **ground almonds**

300 ml (½ pint) **natural yogurt**

300 ml (½ pint) **double cream**

6 tablespoons chopped **fresh coriander**

To serve

plain rice

mango chutney

Heat the oil in a large, heavy-based frying pan and cook the onion and chicken for 5 minutes or until softened and golden in places. Add all the spices and cook over a high heat for a further 2–3 minutes, tossing and stirring until well blended.

Add the ground almonds and stir to coat, then pour in the yogurt and cream. Cook, uncovered and stirring occasionally, over a gentle heat for 10 minutes or until the chicken is cooked and the sauce is well coloured and a good consistency, adding a little water if necessary.

Remove from the heat, stir in the fresh coriander and serve with rice and mango chutney.

For quick chicken korma, heat 2 tablespoons vegetable oil in a large, heavy-based frying pan and cook 500 g (1 lb) diced skinless chicken breast fillets over a high heat, stirring occasionally, for 5 minutes or until golden in places. Add 3 tablespoons korma curry paste and cook for a few seconds before adding 300 g (10 oz) natural yogurt and 8 tablespoons double cream. Cook over a medium-high heat for 4–5 minutes or until the sauce has reduced slightly and the chicken is cooked through. Serve with warmed naan bread. Total cooking time **10 minutes.**

mushroom, herb & chicken frittata

Serves **4**

Total cooking time **20 minutes**

1 tablespoon **olive oil**

1 **skinless chicken breast fillet**, sliced

200 g (7 oz) **mixed mushrooms**, such as chestnut, oyster and shiitake, sliced

1 **red pepper**, cored, deseeded and chopped

4 **spring onions**, sliced

8 **eggs**

3 tablespoons chopped **herbs**, such as parsley, chives and thyme

125 g (4 oz) **low-fat soft cheese with chives**

salt and **pepper**

Heat the oil in a large, nonstick frying pan. Add the chicken, mushrooms, red pepper and spring onions and cook over a high heat, stirring, for 5 minutes or until the chicken is cooked and the vegetables are tender.

Beat the eggs with the herbs and season with salt and pepper. Pour into the pan over the chicken and vegetables and cook gently for about 5 minutes or until set around the edges.

Dot the soft cheese over the top of the frittata and place the pan under a preheated medium grill. Cook until just set and the top is golden. Serve warm or cold.

For garlic mushroom & chicken pizza, heat 1 tablespoon sunflower oil in a large nonstick frying pan and fry 200 g (7 oz) sliced mixed mushrooms in for 3 minutes, then stir in 1 chopped ready-cooked chicken breast. Spread a large ready-made pizza base with ready-made tomato sauce, spoon the mushroom mixture over the top and dot with low-fat garlic and herb soft cheese. Bake in a preheated oven, 220°C (435°F) Gas Mark 7, for 10 minutes or until the cheese is melted and the crust is golden. **Total cooking time 15 minutes.**

meat

easy cassoulet

Serves **4**

Total cooking time **30 minutes**

2 tablespoons **olive oil**

4 **Cumberland sausages**

4 **boneless, skinless chicken thighs**, opened out flat

1 large **onion**, chopped

2 **celery sticks**, chopped

2 teaspoons **sweet smoked paprika**

2 x 400 g (13 oz) cans **chopped tomatoes with garlic and herbs**

2 x 400 g (13 oz) cans **cannellini beans**, rinsed and drained

8 tablespoons **fresh white breadcrumbs**

2 tablespoons chopped **parsley**

salt and **pepper**

Heat 2 tablespoons of the oil in a large saucepan, add the sausages and chicken thighs and fry for 5 minutes, turning occasionally, until browned. Remove the meat from the pan and slice the sausages.

Add the onion and celery to the pan and fry for 2–3 minutes until slightly softened. Add the paprika, stir well and return the sausages and chicken to the pan. Add the tomatoes and beans and season. Bring to the boil, then reduce the heat, cover and simmer for 20 minutes.

Meanwhile, heat the remaining oil in a frying pan, add the breadcrumbs and fry, stirring, until golden.

Serve the cassoulet sprinkled with the breadcrumbs and parsley.

For smoky sausage & beans on toast, heat 2 tablespoons olive oil in a large saucepan, add 2 chopped onions and fry for 5 minutes until softened. Add 2 x 400 g (13 oz) cans baked beans, 2 tablespoons smoky barbecue sauce and 2 teaspoons Dijon mustard, then stir in 250 g (8 oz) sliced smoked pork sausage and heat through. Serve on thick slices of buttered wholemeal toast. **Total cooking time 10 minutes.**

lamb meatballs with feta couscous

Serves **2**

Total cooking time **20 minutes**

200 g (7 oz) **lean minced
  lamb**
1 **garlic clove**, crushed
½ teaspoon **ground cumin**
½ teaspoon **ground coriander**
2 tablespoons **olive oil**
salt and **pepper**
raita or **tzatziki**, to serve

Couscous
125 g (4 oz) **couscous**
1 tablespoon chopped **parsley**
1 tablespoon chopped **mint
  leaves**
50 g (2 oz) **feta cheese**,
  crumbled
75 g (3 oz) **ready-cooked
  fresh beetroot**, chopped

Place the lamb in a bowl, add the garlic, cumin and coriander and season with salt and pepper. Mix well, then, using your hands, shape into 8 meatballs, pressing the mixture together firmly.

Heat the oil in a frying pan, add the meatballs and fry over a medium heat for 8–10 minutes or until browned and cooked through.

Meanwhile, place the couscous in a heatproof bowl and just cover with boiling water. Cover the bowl with clingfilm and leave to stand for 5 minutes. Fluff up the couscous with a fork, then season and stir in the herbs. Lightly stir through the feta and beetroot.

Serve the meatballs with the couscous and generous spoonfuls of raita or tzatziki.

For lamb burgers with herb & feta couscous, soak a 100 g (3½ oz) pack coriander and lemon couscous in boiling water according to the pack instructions. Meanwhile, grill or fry 2 ready-made lamb burgers, about 125 g (4 oz) each, for about 5–8 minutes or until cooked through, turning once. Fluff up the couscous with a fork. Stir in 50 g (2 oz) crumbled feta cheese and 75 g (3 oz) chopped ready-cooked fresh beetroot. Serve with the burgers. **Total cooking time 10 minutes.**

eggs benedict

Serves **2**
Total cooking time **10 minutes**

2 large **eggs**
2 **English muffins**
6 tablespoons **ready-made**
   Hollandaise sauce
2 thick slices of **cooked ham**
salt and **pepper**
chopped **chives**, to garnish

Break the eggs into a saucepan of simmering water and cook for 3–4 minutes for a soft yolk or longer if you prefer your eggs completely set.

Meanwhile, split the muffins and toast them in a toaster or under a preheated hot grill. Gently warm the Hollandaise sauce in a microwaveable bowl in a microwave oven or in a heatproof bowl set over a saucepan of simmering water.

Place the ham on one half of each muffin. Drain the eggs with a slotted spoon and place on the ham. Season, then spoon over the warmed Hollandaise and sprinkle with chives. Top with the remaining muffin halves and serve.

For eggs Benedict with homemade Hollandaise sauce, whisk together 2 egg yolks, 1 teaspoon white wine vinegar and 1 teaspoon lemon juice in a bowl. Gradually add 75 g (3 oz) cooled melted butter, whisking constantly. Season and add extra lemon juice to taste. Make the Eggs Benedict as above. Spoon over the warmed Hollandaise sauce and sprinkle with chives. Total cooking time 20 minutes.

chinese beef stir-fry

Serves **4**

Total cooking time **30 minutes**

2 tablespoons **sunflower oil**

400 g (13 oz) **firm tofu**, cut
   into 1.5 cm (¾ inch) cubes

2 teaspoons peeled and
   grated **fresh root ginger**

6 **spring onions**, chopped,
   plus extra, to garnish

1 **red chilli**, deseeded and
   finely chopped, plus extra,
   to garnish

½ **red pepper**, cored,
   deseeded and cut into thick
   strips

½ **yellow pepper**, cored,
   deseeded and cut into thick
   strips

200 g (7 oz) **shiitake
   mushrooms**, sliced

1 tablespoon **cornflour**

2 tablespoons **dark soy sauce**

2 tablespoons **oyster sauce**

50 ml (2 fl oz) **mirin**

200 ml (7 fl oz) hot **vegetable
   stock**

400 g (13 oz) **ready-cooked
   roast beef slices**, cut into
   strips

steamed **rice**, to serve

Heat the oil in a wok until hot, add the tofu in batches
and stir-fry over a high heat for 3–4 minutes or until
golden. Remove with a slotted spoon and drain on
kitchen paper.

Add the ginger, spring onions, red chilli, red and yellow
peppers and mushrooms to the wok and stir-fry over a
high heat for 3–4 minutes until softened.

Mix the cornflour with a little water in a small bowl
until well blended. Add the soy sauce, oyster sauce,
mirin and stock, and mix well. Add the liquid to the wok
and bring to the boil. Reduce the heat to medium-low,
return the tofu to the wok with the beef strips, toss
to mix well and simmer gently for 2–3 minutes until
heated through.

Ladle into warmed bowls, scatter with sliced spring
onion and red chilli to garnish and serve with steamed
rice.

For Chinese beef, tofu & vegetable salad, core,
deseed and slice 1 red pepper and 1 yellow pepper,
then put in a large salad bowl with 400 g (13 oz)
ready-cooked roast beef slices, thickly sliced, 6 sliced
spring onions and 200 g (7 oz) firm tofu, cubed. Place
1 teaspoon fresh root ginger paste, 1 teaspoon chilli
oil, 1 teaspoon sesame oil, 4 tablespoons sunflower oil
and 6 tablespoons light soy sauce in a bowl. Stir to mix
well, pour the dressing over the salad and serve. Total
cooking time 10 minutes.

chorizo & red pepper tortilla

Serves **4**

Total cooking time **25 minutes**

2 tablespoons **olive oil**

250 g (8 oz) **cooking chorizo**, diced

1 large **red onion**, halved and sliced

2 **garlic cloves**, chopped

1 teaspoon **hot smoked paprika**

½ teaspoon **dried thyme**

1 teaspoon **dried oregano**

375 g (12 oz) **roasted red peppers from a jar**, drained and rinsed, cut into strips

6 **eggs**, lightly beaten

2 tablespoons chopped **flat leaf parsley**

125 g (4 oz) **Cheddar cheese**, grated

pepper

Heat the oil in a large, nonstick frying pan and add the chorizo and onion. Cook gently for 2–3 minutes, then stir in the garlic. Cook for 4–5 minutes until softened. Stir in the spices and dried herbs and cook for a further 2 minutes, then add the peppers.

Beat the eggs with the parsley and season with pepper. Pour the egg mixture into the pan and cook gently for 3–4 minutes, stirring occasionally to prevent the base from burning, until the egg is almost set.

Sprinkle with the grated Cheddar, then slide under a preheated hot grill, keeping the handle away from the heat. Grill for 2–3 minutes until golden and set. Slice into wedges and serve immediately.

For chorizo & red pepper bagels, split 4 bagels and toast until lightly golden. Place, cut side up, on a baking sheet and top with 75 g (3 oz) thinly sliced cured chorizo, 200 g (7 oz) roasted red peppers from a jar, drained and sliced, 125 g (4 oz) grated Cheddar cheese and 1 teaspoon dried oregano. Cook under a preheated hot grill for 4–5 minutes until bubbling. Meanwhile, heat 1 tablespoon olive oil in a frying pan until very hot, and break 4 small eggs into the pan. Fry for 2–3 minutes until the whites are set but the yolks are still runny. Arrange the bagels on 4 plates and top each with a fried egg and a sprinkle of pepper. **Total cooking time 10 minutes.**

special fried rice

Serves **4**

Total cooking time **10 minutes**

2 tablespoons **sesame oil**

2 **eggs**, beaten

8 **rindless streaky bacon rashers**, snipped into pieces

1 bunch of **spring onions**, roughly chopped

100 g (3½ oz) small **cooked peeled prawns**

100 g (3½ oz) **frozen peas**

250 g (8 oz) **ready-cooked long-grain rice**

salt and **pepper**

Heat 1 tablespoon of the oil in a large frying pan, pour in the eggs in a thin layer and cook over a medium heat for 1–2 minutes until golden and set. Remove and cut into shreds.

Add the remaining oil to the pan and stir-fry the bacon and spring onions over a high heat for 2–3 minutes until the bacon is browned and the onions softened. Add the prawns and peas and stir-fry for a further 1 minute. Add the rice and stir-fry for 2–3 minutes until hot.

Stir the shredded omelette into the rice and heat through for a few seconds. Season with salt and pepper and serve immediately.

For stir-fried beef & chilli rice, bring a saucepan of lightly salted water to the boil and cook 200 g (7 oz) easy-cook long-grain rice for 15 minutes until tender, then drain. Meanwhile, heat 1 tablespoon sesame oil in a large wok or heavy-based frying pan and stir-fry 300 g (10 oz) thinly sliced rump steak over a high heat for 3–4 minutes until browned. Add 1 bunch of chopped spring onions and stir-fry for 2 minutes, then add 100 g (3½ oz) peas, defrosted if frozen, and stir-fry for a further 2 minutes until hot. Stir in 75 g (3 oz) chopped toasted cashew nuts, 6 tablespoons chopped fresh coriander and 5 tablespoons sweet chilli sauce and stir-fry for 1 minute to heat through. Add the rice and cook, tossing, for a further 2 minutes. Total cooking time 20 minutes.

lamb chops with spicy chickpeas

Serves **4**

Total cooking time **20 minutes**

2 tablespoons **olive oil**

8 **lamb chops**, about 150 g
(5 oz) each

2 x 400 g (13 oz) **cans
chickpeas**, drained and
rinsed

2 **red chillies**, deseeded and
finely chopped

2 teaspoons **cumin seeds**

1 teaspoon crushed **coriander
seeds**

100 g (3½ oz) **roasted red
peppers from a jar**, drained
and sliced

finely grated rind and juice of
1 **lemon**

400 g (13 oz) **baby spinach
leaves**

small handful of **fresh
coriander leaves**, chopped,
plus extra to garnish

salt and **pepper**

Heat the oil in a large frying pan, add the chops, in batches if necessary, and cook over a medium heat for 2–3 minutes on each side or until cooked to your liking. Remove from the pan, cover with foil and keep warm.

Add the remaining ingredients to the pan, increase the heat to high and cook, stirring, for 4–5 minutes or until piping hot and the spinach has wilted.

Spoon the chickpea mixture into 4 warmed bowls and season to taste. Top with the lamb chops, scatter with extra chopped coriander and serve immediately.

For spicy lamb, spinach & chickpea salad, brush 4 lamb leg steaks, about 150 g (5 oz) each, with 1 tablespoon olive oil, then cook under a preheated hot grill for 2–3 minutes on each side or until cooked to your liking. Put 100 g (3½ oz) baby spinach leaves, 2 chopped tomatoes and a rinsed and drained 400 g (13 oz) can chickpeas in a large salad bowl. Cut the slightly cooled lamb into bite-sized pieces and add to the bowl. Pour over 150 ml (¼ pint) ready-made fresh vinaigrette, then sprinkle over 1 teaspoon hot curry powder and season. Toss to mix well and serve. **Total cooking time 10 minutes**.

bacon & onion pan-cooked tart

Serves **4**

Total cooking time **30 minutes**

500 g (1 lb) **potatoes**, peeled
and thickly sliced

2 tablespoons **olive oil**

250 g (8 oz) **rindless back
bacon**, roughly chopped

1 large **onion**, sliced

250 g (8 oz) tub **ricotta
cheese**

2 **eggs**

4 tablespoons chopped
parsley

600 ml (1 pint) **chicken stock**

salt and **pepper**

salad, to serve (optional)

Bring a large saucepan of lightly salted water to the boil and cook the potatoes for 10 minutes.

Meanwhile, heat the oil in a large, heavy-based frying pan and cook the bacon and onion over a medium heat, stirring frequently, for 5 minutes until the bacon has browned and the onion softened.

Drain the potatoes well, then add to the frying pan and cook, stirring frequently without worrying if the potatoes break up, for 2 minutes.

Dot spoonfuls of the ricotta over the potato mixture. Beat the eggs and parsley into the stock in a bowl, season with pepper and pour over the potato mixture. Cook gently for 10 minutes, then cook under a preheated hot grill for a further 2–3 minutes until golden and set.

Serve spooned on to warmed serving plates, with a simple salad, if liked.

For chorizo, spinach & onion omelette, tip 400 g (13 oz) spinach leaves into a colander and slowly pour a kettleful of boiling water over until wilted. Cool under cold running water, then squeeze out all the liquid. Heat 3 tablespoons olive oil in a large frying pan and cook 1 finely chopped onion and 100 g (3½ oz) sliced cured chorizo over a medium heat, stirring, for 5 minutes. Beat 6 large eggs in a bowl, season and stir in the spinach. Pour over the chorizo mixture and cook for 4 minutes, then cook under a preheated hot grill for 1 minute to set the top. **Total cooking time 15 minutes.**

mushroom & cheese burgers

Serves **4**

Total cooking time **20 minutes**

500 g (1 lb) **minced steak**

1 teaspoon **sweet smoked paprika**

4 **spring onions**, thinly sliced

1 **egg yolk**, beaten

1 teaspoon **prepared English mustard**

1 tablespoon **olive oil**

4 **chestnut mushrooms**, sliced

4 **good-quality wholemeal buns**

4 slices of **Emmental** or **Gruyère cheese**

Salsa

½ **cucumber**, roughly chopped

2 tablespoons chopped **fresh coriander**

pepper

Place the minced steak in a bowl with the paprika, spring onions, egg yolk and mustard and mix together with a fork until thoroughly blended. Using your hands, shape into 4 patties.

Cook the burgers under a preheated hot grill for 10 minutes, turning once, until they are well browned and cooked through.

Meanwhile, heat the oil in a large, heavy-based frying pan and cook the mushrooms over a high heat, stirring frequently, for 5 minutes until browned.

Make the salsa by simply tossing the cucumber and coriander together, and season with a little pepper.

Split each roll and serve a burger in each, topped with a slice of cheese to melt, then the mushrooms and a spoonful of salsa.

For quick & healthy mini burgers, mix together 300 g (10 oz) lean minced beef, 50 g (2 oz) fresh wholemeal breadcrumbs, 50 g (2 oz) grated carrot, 1 small grated onion, 1 crushed garlic clove, a handful of chopped parsley and 2 teaspoons Worcestershire sauce. Shape the mixture into 8 small patties and cook under a preheated medium grill for 3 minutes on each side until cooked through. Serve in split, toasted wholemeal mini buns with a spoonful of ready-made fresh tomato salsa. **Total cooking time 10 minutes.**

honey & mustard pork chops

Serves **4**

Total cooking time **10 minutes**

1 tablespoon **clear honey**

1 tablespoon **wholegrain mustard**

4 small **pork chops**, about 175 g (6 oz) each

100 g (3½ oz) pack **instant mashed potato**

3 tablespoons **crème fraîche**

50 g (2 oz) **butter**

200 g (7 oz) **spinach leaves**

pepper

Mix together the honey and mustard, then brush over the chops. Cook under a preheated medium grill for 3–4 minutes on each side or until cooked through.

Meanwhile, make up the instant mash according to the pack instructions, season with pepper and mix in the crème fraîche.

Melt the butter in a large saucepan and cook the spinach over a medium heat, stirring, for 2 minutes until just wilted.

Stir the spinach into the mash and serve with the grilled pork chops.

For creamy pork & mustard with instant mash, heat 2 tablespoons olive oil in a large, heavy-based frying pan and cook 4 thinly sliced pork steaks and 2 red onions, cut into slim wedges, over a medium heat, stirring occasionally, for 7–8 minutes until the pork is browned and cooked through and the onion is tender. Add 150 ml (¼ pint) cider, bring to the boil and continue boiling for 2 minutes until the liquid has reduced by half. Add 200 ml (7 fl oz) crème fraîche and 1 tablespoon wholegrain mustard and season well with salt and pepper. Heat through for 2–3 minutes, then stir in 3 tablespoons chopped parsley. Serve with instant mash, prepared according to the pack instructions. **Total cooking time 20 minutes.**

spicy beef enchilada wraps

Serves **4**

Total cooking time **10 minutes**

8 **corn tortillas**

8 tablespoons **hot chilli sauce**

8 tablespoons **ready-made guacamole**, plus extra to serve

8 tablespoons **soured cream**, plus extra to serve

¼ **iceberg lettuce**, shredded

400 g (13 oz) **ready-cooked roast beef slices**, thickly sliced

8 tablespoons **sliced green jalapeño chillies from a jar**, drained

8 tablespoons **ready-made fresh tomato salsa**

salt and **pepper**

Place 1 tortilla on a hot griddle or in a hot dry frying pan and cook according to the pack instructions until heated through. Remove and keep warm, then repeat with the remaining tortillas.

Lay the tortillas on a clean work surface and spread each one with 1 tablespoon each of the hot chilli sauce, guacamole and soured cream. Divide the lettuce between the tortillas, then top with the roast beef and 1 tablespoon each of the jalapeños and salsa. Season well.

Roll up the filled tortillas to form wraps and serve immediately with extra guacamole and soured cream.

For spicy enchilada beef rice, heat 2 tablespoons sunflower oil in a large frying pan, add 1 chopped onion and 400 g (13 oz) minced beef and fry, stirring, over a high heat for 6–8 minutes until browned. Stir in a 375 g (12 oz) jar enchilada sauce and cook for 2–3 minutes or until bubbling. Add 500 g (1 lb) ready-cooked long-grain rice and continue to stir and cook for 3–4 minutes or until piping hot. Season and serve immediately. **Total cooking time 20 minutes.**

lamb & tray-roasted vegetables

Serves **4**

Total cooking time **25 minutes**

1 tablespoon **olive oil**

8 **lamb chops**

1 **aubergine**, trimmed and cut into cubes

1 large **red onion**, cut into chunks

2 **courgettes**, trimmed and cut into chunks

1 **red pepper**, cored, deseeded and cut into chunks

1 **yellow pepper**, cored, deseeded and cut into chunks

375 g (12 oz) **tomatoes**, cut into quarters

1 teaspoon **ground cumin**

1 teaspoon **ground coriander**

400 g (13 oz) can **chickpeas**, drained

3 tablespoons **pumpkin seeds**

Heat the oil in a large, heavy-based frying pan and cook the lamb chops over a high heat for 1 minute on each side until browned and sealed. Transfer to a large roasting tin with a fish slice, reserving the cooking juices in the pan, and place in a preheated oven, 220°C (425°F), Gas Mark 7, while pan-frying the vegetables.

Add the aubergine, onion, courgettes and peppers to the frying pan and cook over a high heat, stirring frequently, for 5 minutes. Add the tomatoes and cook, stirring, for 2 minutes.

Transfer all the vegetables to the roasting tin with the lamb, add the spices and chickpeas and toss to mix. Return to the top shelf of the oven for a further 10 minutes or until the lamb is cooked through.

Scatter over the pumpkin seeds before serving.

For pesto lamb & vegetable bake, prepare the recipe as above, but instead of flavouring the lamb and vegetables with cumin and coriander, make your own green pesto instead. In a food processor, whizz together a handful of basil leaves, 3 tablespoons olive oil, the juice of 1 lemon, 25 g (1 oz) freshly grated Parmesan cheese and 75 g (3 oz) pine nuts until smooth. Toss the pesto into the roasting tin with the lamb, pan-fried vegetables and chickpeas, and bake as above. **Total cooking time 30 minutes.**

creamy coconut beef rendang

Serves **4**

Total cooking time **20 minutes**

250 g (8 oz) **Thai jasmine rice**

2 tablespoons **vegetable oil**

1 tablespoon peeled and finely chopped **fresh root ginger**

1 **bird's eye chilli**, thinly sliced

1 **garlic clove**, thinly sliced

1 **lemon grass stalk**, thinly sliced

500 g (1 lb) **frying steak**, cut into strips

½ teaspoon **ground cinnamon**

pinch of **ground turmeric**

juice of 1 **lime**

400 g (13 oz) can **reduced-fat coconut milk**

4 tablespoons chopped **fresh coriander**

Cook the jasmine rice, according to the pack instructions.

Meanwhile, heat the oil in a large, heavy-based frying pan or wok and cook the ginger, chilli, garlic and lemon grass over a medium heat, stirring frequently, for 1–2 minutes until softened but not coloured. Add the beef, increase the heat to high and stir-fry for 5 minutes until browned and cooked through.

Stir in the cinnamon and turmeric and cook, stirring, for a few seconds before adding the lime juice and coconut milk. Gently heat, stirring, for 2–3 minutes until the sauce is hot.

Serve immediately with the cooked jasmine rice and scattered with the chopped coriander.

For speedy Thai-style beef & coconut skewers,
cut 500 g (1 lb) fillet steak into chunks. Thread on to 8 metal skewers alternately with 2 red peppers, cored, deseeded and cut into chunky pieces. Mix 4 tablespoons Thai red curry paste with 200 ml (7 fl oz) coconut cream and spoon over the skewers. Cook under a preheated hot grill for 3–4 minutes on each side or until cooked through. Serve with warmed pitta bread. **Total cooking time 10 minutes.**

spaghetti carbonara

Serves **4**

Total cooking time **10 minutes**

400 g (13 oz) **dried spaghetti**
150 g (5 oz) **streaky bacon
  rashers**
2 **egg yolks**
4 tablespoons **double cream**
25 g (1 oz) **Parmesan
  cheese**, grated, plus extra
  to serve
salt and **pepper**
green salad, to serve

Cook the pasta in a large saucepan of salted boiling water according to the pack instructions until al dente.

Meanwhile, cook the bacon under a preheated medium grill for 7 minutes or until crisp. Cool for 1 minute, then cut into small pieces.

Mix together the egg yolks, cream and Parmesan in a bowl.

Drain the pasta, reserving a little of the cooking water, and return to the pan. Stir in the bacon and cream mixture, adding a little cooking water to loosen if needed. Season well.

Pile on to serving plates, scatter with extra Parmesan and serve with a green salad.

For spaghetti carbonara with poached eggs, crack 1 egg into a small cup. Bring a shallow pan of water to the boil, stir the water vigorously to make a whirlpool, then gently slide the egg into the centre. Leave to cook for 3 minutes, then lift out with a slotted spoon, pat dry with kitchen paper and keep warm. Repeat with 3 more eggs. Meanwhile, make the recipe as above and serve topped with the eggs. **Total cooking time 15 minutes.**

stir-fried beef & leeks

Serves **4**
Total cooking time **15 minutes**

2 tablespoons **sunflower oil**
400 g (13 oz) **sirloin steak**,
  cut into strips
2 **garlic cloves**, crushed
1 teaspoon **dried chilli flakes**
4 **leeks**, trimmed, cleaned and
  thinly sliced
juice of 1 **lemon**
2 tablespoons **crème fraîche**
salt and **pepper**
steamed **broccoli**, to serve

Heat the oil in a wok or large frying pan until hot, add the beef and stir-fry for 2 minutes. Remove from the pan with a slotted spoon.

Add the garlic, chilli flakes and leeks to the pan and stir-fry for 3–4 minutes.

Return the beef to the pan, then stir in the lemon juice and crème fraîche and cook for about 2 minutes until heated through.

Season to taste and serve with steamed broccoli.

For beef steak & caramelized leek sandwiches,

heat 25 g (1 oz) butter and 1 tablespoon olive oil in a frying pan, add 2 trimmed, cleaned and sliced leeks and cook over a low heat for 10 minutes, stirring occasionally. Add 1 tablespoon soft dark brown sugar and 1 tablespoon white wine and cook for a further 5 minutes. Meanwhile, heat a griddle pan until smoking hot, add 4 sirloin steaks, about 150 g (5 oz) each, and cook for 3–4 minutes on each side or until cooked to your liking. Leave to rest. Toast 4 split ciabatta rolls, then spread the bases with 1 teaspoon horseradish sauce mixed with 1 tablespoon mayonnaise. Top each with a steak and the caramelized leeks, then add the lids and serve. **Total cooking time 20 minutes.**

sage liver & mash

Serves **4**
Total cooking time **10 minutes**

625 g (1¼ lb) **shop-bought
  ready-made mashed
  potatoes**
450 g (14½ oz) **lambs' liver**,
  thinly sliced
2 tablespoons **flour**, seasoned
50 g (2 oz) **butter**
4–5 **sage leaves**, chopped

Warm the mash according to the pack instructions.

Meanwhile, dust the lambs' liver in the seasoned flour.

Heat the butter in a frying pan and cook the liver with the sage leaves for 1–2 minutes on each side.

Serve with the warmed mashed potatoes, pouring the butter and juices over the potatoes.

For lambs' liver with mushrooms, dust 450 g (14½ oz) lambs' liver with 2 tablespoons plain flour seasoned with salt and pepper. Heat 1 tablespoon olive oil in a frying pan and cook the liver for 2 minutes on each side. Remove and keep warm. Heat another 1 tablespoon olive oil in a clean frying pan and sauté 1 sliced onion and 150 g (5 oz) sliced chestnut mushrooms for 4–5 minutes. Meanwhile, bring 750 ml (1¼ pints) water to the boil in a saucepan. Pour in 200 g (7 oz) instant polenta and cook for 1–2 minutes, stirring contantly, until it thickens. Prepare 1 tablespoon chopped chives and 1 tablespoon chopped parsley and stir half of these into the polenta. Add the remaining herbs to the mushroom mixture and then add the liver and the juice of 1 lemon and heat for 1 minute. Serve the liver and mushrooms spooned over the herb polenta. **Total cooking time 20 minutes.**

cajun-spiced hot dogs

Serves **4**

Total cooking time **10 minutes**

2 tablespoons **vegetable oil**

1 **red onion**, halved and sliced

2 **red peppers**, or **1 red** and
   1 yellow, cored, deseeded
   and sliced

8 **chicken** or **pork frankfurter
   sausages**

1 tablespoon **Cajun
   seasoning mix**

To serve

8 **long bread rolls**, warmed

ready-made tomato salsa
   (optional)

Heat the oil in a large, nonstick frying pan and cook the onion and peppers over a high heat for 6–7 minutes until slightly charred.

Reduce the heat slightly and add the frankfurters and Cajun spices. Cook for 2–3 minutes, until hot.

Serve the sausages and cooked vegetables in the split warmed rolls with salsa, if liked.

For Cajun-spiced sausage fajitas, cook 8 pork sausages under a preheated medium grill for 12 minutes, turning frequently, until cooked through and golden. Meanwhile, heat 2 tablespoons vegetable oil in a frying pan, and cook 1 halved and sliced red onion and 2 cored, deseeded and sliced red peppers over a high heat for 6–7 minutes, until slightly charred. Thickly slice the sausages diagonally, add to the pan with 1 tablespoon Cajun seasoning mix and cook, stirring frequently for 2–3 minutes until the sausages are golden. Divide the mixture between 4–8 soft flour tortillas. Top with 150 g (5 oz) grated Cheddar cheese, 1 small tomato, shredded Iceberg lettuce and some ready-made salsa. Roll up the tortillas, cut in half and serve immediately. **Total cooking time 20 minutes.**

mustard & cheese grilled gammon

Serves **4**

Total cooking time **15 minutes**

1 tablespoon **vegetable oil**

4 **thick gammon steaks**, about 175 g (6 oz) each

2 tablespoons **wholegrain mustard**

2 tablespoons chopped **mixed herbs**, such as parsley, chives, thyme and oregano

75 g (3 oz) **Cheddar cheese**, grated

2 tablespoons **onion chutney** or 2 **spring onions**, finely sliced

To serve

crusty bread

mixed salad leaves

Rub the oil over the gammon steaks and arrange on a foil-lined grill rack. Cook under a preheated hot grill for 4–5 minutes on each side until cooked through.

Meanwhile, mix the mustard with the chopped herbs, grated cheese and onion chutney or spring onions.

Spoon the mixture on to the gammon steaks, return to the grill and cook under a medium heat for a further 3–4 minutes until melted and golden.

Serve with crusty bread and mixed salad leaves.

For ham & mustard croque monsieur, mix 150 g (5 oz) coarsely grated Cheddar cheese in a bowl with 2 tablespoons mayonnaise, 1 tablespoon wholegrain mustard and 2 tablespoons chopped mixed herbs (as above), then spread over 4 slices of sandwich bread. Top with 4 slices of cooked ham and cover each with a second piece of bread. Heat gently in a large, nonstick frying pan for 6–7 minutes, turning once, until the bread is golden brown and the inside is hot and melted. Serve cut in half with salad leaves and onion chutney. **Total cooking time 10 minutes.**

spicy lamb tagine

Serves **4**

Total cooking time **30 minutes**

2 tablespoons **olive oil**

750 g (1½ lb) **boneless shoulder of lamb**, cut into cubes

1 **onion**, chopped

1 **garlic clove**, crushed

1 teaspoon **ground cumin**

1 teaspoon **ground cinnamon**

½ teaspoon **ground ginger**

500 ml (17 fl oz) **chicken stock**

2 tablespoons **tomato purée**

1 teaspoon **soft dark brown sugar**

75 g (3 oz) **ready-to eat dried apricots**

50 g (2 oz) **prunes**

50 g (2 oz) **flaked almonds**, toasted

cooked **quinoa**, to serve

Heat the oil in a large, flameproof casserole dish over a medium heat and brown the meat (you may have to do this in batches), then remove with a slotted spoon and set aside.

Add the onion and garlic to the pan and cook for 2–3 minutes, then stir in the spices and cook for a further minute.

Return the lamb to the pan with the stock, tomato purée, sugar and dried fruit. Bring to the boil, then simmer for 25 minutes.

Serve sprinkled with toasted flaked almonds, with cooked quinoa.

For spiced lamb chops with quinoa salad, cook 100 g (3½ oz) quinoa in boiling water for 8–9 minutes. Meanwhile, mix together 2 teaspoons each ground turmeric, ground cumin and ground cinnamon and 1 teaspoon ground ginger. Rub the spice mixture over 4 lamb chops, about 150 g (5 oz) each, then cook on a hot griddle pan for 3–4 minutes on each side. While the chops are cooking, mix together 2 tablespoons chopped parsley, 1 tablespoon chopped mint, 50 g (2 oz) chopped ready-to-eat dried apricots and 2 tablespoons toasted flaked almonds. Drain the quinoa, then stir in the herb mixture and serve with the lamb chops. **Total cooking time 15 minutes.**

pork escalopes with peperonata

Serves **4**

Total cooking time **30 minutes**

2 tablespoons **olive oil**

1 **onion**, finely diced

2 **garlic cloves**, crushed

2 **red peppers**, cored, deseeded and thinly sliced

1 **yellow pepper**, cored, deseeded and thinly sliced

2 tablespoons **white wine**

400 g (13 oz) can **chopped tomatoes**

4 **pork escalopes**, about 150 g (5 oz) each

1 tablespoon chopped **oregano**

steamed **purple sprouting broccoli**, to serve

Heat 1 tablespoon of the olive oil in a frying pan and sauté the onion for 3–4 minutes. Add the garlic and cook for a further 1 minute.

Stir in the peppers and wine, bring to a simmer, cover and cook for 10 minutes.

Pour in the chopped tomatoes and cook, uncovered, for a further 10–15 minutes until the peppers are soft.

Meanwhile, toss the pork escalopes in the remaining olive oil and the oregano and cook on a hot griddle pan or barbecue for 3–4 minutes on each side.

Serve the escalopes on a bed of the peperonata, with steamed purple sprouting broccoli.

For pork chops with Italian purple sprouting broccoli, cook 625 g (1¼ lb) purple sprouting broccoli in a saucepan of boiling water for 4–5 minutes. Drain. Meanwhile, dust 4 pork escalopes with plain flour seasoned with salt and pepper. Heat 50 g (2 oz) butter and 1 tablespoon olive oil in a frying pan and cook the dusted escalopes with 2 teaspoons chopped sage leaves for 4–5 minutes until cooked through. Heat 2 tablespoons olive oil in a frying pan, add the broccoli and cook for 1 minute. Add 2 chopped garlic cloves, ¼ teaspoon dried chilli flakes, the juice of ½ lemon and some pepper and cook for a further 1 minute. Serve with the pork. **Total cooking time 10 minutes.**

sausages with celeriac mash

Serves **4**

Total cooking time **20 minutes**

625 g (1¼ lb) **floury
  potatoes**, peeled and diced
400 g (13 oz) **celeriac**, peeled
  and diced
8 **country-style pork and
  herb sausages**
50 g (2 oz) **butter**
1 tablespoon chopped **thyme
  leaves**
salt and **pepper**
steamed **carrots**, to serve

Cook the potato and celeriac in a large saucepan of lightly salted boiling water for about 15 minutes until tender. Drain, then return to the pan and place over a low heat for 30 seconds to remove the excess liquid.

Meanwhile, cook the sausages under a preheated medium grill for 12–15 minutes, turning occasionally, until cooked through and golden.

Mash the potato and celeriac with the butter, thyme and plenty of seasoning. Serve the grilled sausages with the mash and some steamed carrots.

For herby sausages with celeriac remoulade, heat 1 tablespoon olive or vegetable oil in a frying pan and cook 12 pork and herb chipolatas for about 8 minutes, turning occasionally, until cooked through and golden. Meanwhile, coarsely grate 575 g (1 lb 3 oz) peeled celeriac and toss with 1 tablespoon lemon juice. Add 5 tablespoons mayonnaise, 2 tablespoons wholegrain mustard and a pinch of sugar, season to taste and mix well to combine. Spoon on to plates and serve with the cooked sausages. **Total cooking time 10 minutes.**

lamb-stuffed pittas

Serves **4**

Total cooking time **10 minutes**

25 g (1 oz) **rocket leaves**

20 **green olives**, pitted and sliced

2 **red peppers**, cored, deseeded and sliced

2 **avocados**, stoned, peeled and chopped

2 **tomatoes**, chopped

4 **spring onions**, sliced

1 tablespoon **ready-made Italian salad dressing**

4 **pitta breads**

300 g (10 oz) **leftover** or **ready-cooked lamb**, sliced

Mix together the rocket leaves, olives, red peppers, avocados, tomatoes and spring onions in a bowl.

Toss in the Italian salad dressing.

Cook the pitta breads under a preheated hot grill for 1–2 minutes. While they are still warm, run a knife down one side and split them open to make 4 pockets.

Divide the cooked lamb between each pitta and then spoon in the salad to serve.

For meat-topped pizzas, heat 1 tablespoon olive oil in a frying pan and sauté 1 diced onion, 1 cored, deseeded and sliced red pepper and 2 crushed garlic cloves for 1–2 minutes. Stir in 400 g (13 oz) minced beef and brown the meat, stirring. Add a 400 g (13 oz) can chopped tomatoes and 2 tablespoons tomato purée and simmer for 3–4 minutes. Spoon the mixture over 4 ready-made pizza bases on a large baking sheet, sprinkle with 300 g (10 oz) grated mozzarella cheese and bake in a preheated oven, 220°C (425°F), Gas Mark 7, for 11–12 minutes, until golden. **Total cooking time 25 minutes.**

fish & seafood

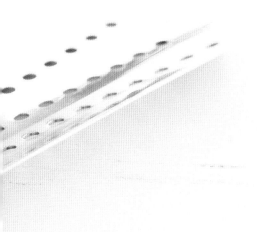

spanish-style baked cod parcels

Serves **4**
Total cooking time **20 minutes**

4 **cod fillets**
400 g (13 oz) can **butter
  beans**, rinsed and drained
125 g (4 oz) **cherry tomatoes**,
  halved
4 **thyme sprigs**
4 **thin cured chorizo slices**
75 ml (3 fl oz) **dry white wine**
salt and **pepper**

Cut 4 large sheets of nonstick baking parchment and place a cod fillet on each. Divide the beans, tomatoes and thyme between the parcels and season well.

Place a chorizo slice on top of each piece of fish and season with salt and pepper, then fold the paper over and roll up the edges to create airtight parcels, leaving just a little gap.

Pour a little of the wine into each parcel and then fully seal, leaving enough space in the packages for air to circulate. Place on a baking sheet and cook in a preheated oven, 220°C (425°F), Gas Mark 7, for 15 minutes until the fish is cooked through.

For seared cod with bean & tomato salad, rub 1 tablespoon olive oil over 4 cod fillets and season well. Place skin side down on a hot griddle pan and cook for 5 minutes. Turn over and cook for a further 3 minutes until golden and cooked through. Meanwhile, whisk together 1 tablespoon balsamic vinegar and 3 tablespoons olive oil. Add 250 g (8 oz) halved cherry tomatoes and a 400 g (13 oz) can butter beans, rinsed and drained. Season to taste and add 100 g (3½ oz) rocket leaves and ½ chopped red chilli. Serve the salad with the cod. **Total cooking time 10 minutes.**

warm bang bang prawn salad

Serves **4**

Total cooking time **20 minutes**

100 g (3½ oz) **dried Thai rice noodles**

finely grated rind and juice of 1 **lime**

1 tablespoon **sesame oil**

125 g (4 oz) **mangetout**

1 **bird's eye chilli**, thinly sliced

2.5 cm (1 inch) piece of **fresh root ginger**, peeled and roughly chopped

250 g (8 oz) large **cooked peeled prawns**

4 tablespoons **smooth peanut butter**

4 tablespoons **light soy sauce**

150 ml (¼ pint) boiling **water**

50 g (2 oz) **dried pineapple pieces**, roughly chopped

Place the noodles in a heatproof bowl, cover with boiling water and leave to soak following the pack instructions until tender. Drain well and toss with the lime rind.

Meanwhile, heat the oil in a large wok or heavy-based frying pan and stir-fry the mangetout, chilli and ginger over a high heat for 2 minutes. Add the prawns and stir-fry for 2 minutes or until hot. Place the peanut butter, lime juice and soy sauce in a jug, add the measurement water and mix well. Pour into the pan and toss the ingredients together.

Add the drained noodles and pineapple pieces and gently toss to coat all the ingredients in the sauce. Serve immediately in warmed serving bowls.

For bang bang skewered prawns, thread each of 8 small metal skewers with 3 large raw peeled prawns. Cook under a preheated hot grill for 3 minutes on each side until they have turned pink. Meanwhile, in a jug, mix 4 tablespoons each smooth peanut butter and light soy sauce with the juice of 1 lime. Serve the sauce in small, individual bowls alongside the skewered prawns and 2 peeled carrots, 2 celery sticks and ½ large cucumber, cut into matchsticks. **Total cooking time 10 minutes.**

trout & bacon hash

Serves **3–4**

Total cooking time **20 minutes**

500 g (1 lb) **new potatoes**, halved

15 g (½ oz) **butter**

375 g (12 oz) **trout fillets**

4 **streaky bacon rashers**

3 tablespoons **olive oil**

1 **onion**, thinly sliced

salt and **pepper**

handful of **flat leaf parsley**, chopped, to garnish

Cook the potatoes in a saucepan of lightly salted boiling water for about 10 minutes until just tender, then drain.

Meanwhile, dot the butter over the trout, season and cook under a preheated hot grill for 7–10 minutes until cooked through. Remove from the grill and set aside, keeping the grill on.

Cook the bacon under the grill until crispy. When the fish is cool enough to handle, discard the skin and break the flesh into large flakes.

Heat 2 tablespoons of the oil in a large frying pan. Add the onion and cook for 5 minutes until softened. Add the remaining oil to the frying pan and add the potatoes. Cook until browned and crisp all over. Break the bacon into pieces, add to the pan with the trout and heat through. Serve scattered with the parsley.

For bacon & smoked trout gnocchi, cook 4 streaky bacon rashers under a preheated hot grill until crispy. Meanwhile, cook 400 g (13 oz) fresh potato gnocchi according to the pack instructions. Drain and mix with 150 g (5 oz) skinless smoked trout fillets, broken into chunks, 1 teaspoon wholegrain mustard and 2 tablespoons olive oil. Crumble over the bacon to serve. **Total cooking time 10 minutes.**

smoked haddock & corn chowder

Serves **4**

Total cooking time **20 minutes**

15 g (½ oz) **butter**

1 small **onion**, chopped

600 ml (1 pint) **milk**

50 ml (2 fl oz) **double cream**

375 g (12 oz) **new potatoes**, halved

3 **streaky bacon rashers**, chopped

2 **skinless smoked haddock fillets**, about 150 g (5 oz) each

125 g (4 oz) drained canned **sweetcorn kernels**

salt and **pepper**

handful of **chives**, chopped, to garnish

crusty bread, to serve

Melt the butter in a large, heavy-based saucepan. Add the onion and cook for a few minutes until softened. Pour over the milk and cream, add the potatoes and season. Bring to the boil and cook for 10 minutes.

Meanwhile, cook the bacon under a preheated hot grill for 7–10 minutes until crisp, then set aside.

Add the fish fillets to the milk and potato mixture and cook for 3 minutes. Stir through the sweetcorn, gently breaking up the fish, and cook for a further 3 minutes or until the fish is cooked through.

Ladle into serving bowls, then crumble over the bacon and scatter with the chives. Serve with crusty bread.

For griddled haddock & creamed corn, heat a griddle pan until smoking hot. Rub 1 tablespoon vegetable oil over 4 haddock fillets, about 150 g (5 oz) each. Cook in the pan, skin side down, for 5 minutes. Turn over and cook for a further 3 minutes until cooked through. Meanwhile, heat 25 g (1 oz) butter in a saucepan. Add a drained 200 g (7 oz) can sweetcorn kernels and heat through. Stir in 3 tablespoons crème fraîche. Scatter over a handful of chives, chopped, and serve with the haddock. **Total cooking time 10 minutes.**

grilled hake with bacon & lemon

Serves **4**
Total cooking time **10 minutes**

2 tablespoons **olive oil**
4 **hake steaks**, about 175 g
  (6 oz) each
25 g (1 oz) **butter**
2 **streaky bacon rashers**,
  finely sliced
finely grated rind and juice of
  1 **lemon**
handful of **flat leaf parsley**,
  chopped
salt and **pepper**

Rub 1 tablespoon of the oil over the hake steaks and season. Cook on a smoking-hot griddle pan for 5 minutes. Turn over and cook for a further 3 minutes until just cooked through.

Meanwhile, heat the remaining oil in a frying pan with the butter. Add the bacon and cook for 5–7 minutes until crispy. Stir in the lemon rind and juice and the parsley.

Place the fish on warmed serving plates and spoon over the sauce.

For fish finger & bacon sandwich, place 8 fish fingers on a baking sheet in a preheated oven, 230°C (450°F), Gas Mark 8, for 12–15 minutes until crisp and brown, turning halfway through cooking. Meanwhile, cook 4 streaky bacon rashers under a preheated hot grill for 5 minutes on each side until crisp. Mix together the juice of ½ lemon and 4 tablespoons mayonnaise. Spread the mayonnaise over 4 slices of white bread. Top each bread slice with 2 fish fingers, a bacon rasher and a handful of chopped lettuce. Cover with another slice of bread and serve with some crisps.
Total cooking time 20 minutes.

crab linguine

Serves **4**
Total cooking time **15 minutes**

450 g (14½ oz) **dried linguine**
125 ml (4 fl oz) **olive oil**
2 **garlic cloves**, crushed
1 **red chilli**, deseeded and
  finely diced
grated rind and juice of
  1 **lemon**
250 g (8 oz) **fresh white
  crab meat**
2 tablespoons chopped
  parsley

Cook the linguine in a large saucepan of boiling water according to the pack instructions until al dente.

Meanwhile, in another large saucepan, heat the olive oil and cook the garlic, chilli and lemon rind over a low heat for 3–4 minutes.

Drain the pasta and add it to the olive oil pan along with the lemon juice, crab meat and the chopped parsley. Toss together gently to warm the crab through, and then serve.

For crab pasta salad, cook 300 g (10 oz) fresh fusilli in a saucepan of boiling water according to the pack instructions until al dente, then drain and refresh under cold water. Meanwhile, steam 125 g (4 oz) broccoli florets until just tender, then drain and refresh under cold water. Place the pasta and broccoli in a salad bowl and toss together with 1 cored, deseeded and sliced red pepper, 4 sliced spring onions, 2 chopped plum tomatoes and 250 g (8 oz) fresh white crab meat. Toss together with some ready-made Italian salad dressing and serve with crusty bread. **Total cooking time 10 minutes.**

red mullet with orange couscous

Serves **4**

Total cooking time **20 minutes**

4 **red mullet fillets**, about 150 g (5 oz) each

4 tablespoons **olive oil**, plus extra for oiling

finely grated rind and juice of **1 orange**, plus 1 whole **orange**

4 **thyme sprigs**

375 g (12 oz) **couscous**

400 ml (14 fl oz) hot **vegetable stock**

finely grated rind and juice of ½ **lemon**

100 g (3½ oz) **radishes**, thinly sliced

75 g (3 oz) **pitted black olives**, chopped

handful of **flat leaf parsley**, chopped

salt and **pepper**

Place the fish fillets on a lightly oiled baking sheet. Season well, then drizzle over 1 tablespoon of the oil and a little of the orange juice and scatter with the thyme sprigs. Place in a preheated oven, 180°C (350°F), Gas Mark 4, for 15 minutes until just cooked through.

Meanwhile, place the couscous in a large bowl. Pour over the hot stock, cover and leave for 5–10 minutes until all the liquid is absorbed and the couscous has swelled. Add the orange and lemon rind with a little more of the orange juice, the lemon juice and the remaining oil, then leave to cool.

Peel the remaining orange, discarding any white pith, then cut into small pieces and stir through with a fork, breaking up any clumps. Season and add the radishes, olives and parsley just before serving with the fish.

For red mullet with orange & olive dressing, heat a griddle pan until smoking hot. Brush 2 tablespoons olive oil over 4 red mullet fillets, about 125 g (4 oz) each, and season well. Cook on the pan for 3–5 minutes until just cooked through. Toss together the finely grated rind of ½ orange, juice of ½ lemon, 3 tablespoons olive oil and 25 g (1 oz) chopped pitted black olives. Spoon over the fish to serve. **Total cooking time 10 minutes.**

chilli & coriander crab cakes

Serves **4**

Total cooking time **30 minutes**

400 g (13 oz) **fresh white crabmeat**

200 g (7 oz) **raw peeled tiger prawns**, roughly chopped

1 tablespoon **hot curry paste**

2 **garlic cloves**, very finely chopped

1 **red chilli**, deseeded and finely chopped

1 **red onion**, finely chopped

4 tablespoons chopped **fresh coriander leaves**, plus extra to garnish

1 small **egg**, beaten

100 g (3½ oz) **fresh white breadcrumbs**

sunflower oil, for brushing

salt and **pepper**

To serve
lemon wedges
crisp green salad leaves

Put the crabmeat, prawns, curry paste, garlic, red chilli, red onion, coriander, egg and breadcrumbs in a food processor or blender. Season well, then blend for a few seconds until well mixed. Transfer to a bowl and then, using your hands, combine further to make a thick patty-like mixture.

Line a baking sheet with nonstick baking parchment and brush with a little oil. Using wet hands, divide the crab mixture into 12 equal portions and shape each one into a round cake. Transfer to the prepared baking sheet, brush with a little oil and bake in a preheated oven, 200°C (400°F), Gas Mark 6, for 15–20 minutes or until lightly browned and cooked through.

Transfer to 4 serving plates and serve with lemon wedges to squeeze over and crisp green salad leaves.

For warm crab & chilli rice salad, heat a large nonstick wok or frying pan until hot, add 400 g (13 oz) ready-cooked long-grain rice and stir-fry over a high heat for 3–4 minutes or until piping hot. Remove from the heat and stir in 400 g (13 oz) fresh cooked white crab meat, a handful of chopped fresh coriander and a small handful of chopped mint. Transfer to a large serving dish. Mix together 1 deseeded and diced red chilli, 6 tablespoons olive oil and the juice of 2 limes, then season. Pour the dressing over the salad, toss to mix and serve. **Total cooking time 10 minutes.**

smoked trout pasta with dill sauce

Serves **4**

Total cooking time **10 minutes**

400 g (13 oz) **fresh linguine**

6 tablespoons **crème fraîche**

squeeze of **lemon juice**

handful of **dill**, finely chopped, plus extra to serve

2 **skinless smoked trout fillets**, about 125 g (4 oz) each

2 **spring onions**, chopped

salt and **pepper**

Cook the linguine according to the pack instructions.

Meanwhile, mix together the crème fraîche, lemon juice and dill to make a smooth sauce. Break the trout into bite-sized pieces.

Drain the pasta, reserving a little of the cooking water. Return to the pan and stir through the sauce, trout and spring onions. Season well and add a little of the reserved cooking water to loosen. Serve immediately with extra dill scattered over.

For potato rösti with smoked trout, cook 2 peeled large floury potatoes in a saucepan of boiling water for 5 minutes. Cool under cold running water and pat dry. Roughly grate, squeezing over a little lemon juice to prevent discoloration. Using your hands, squeeze out any excess liquid and form into small cake shapes. Dust with plain flour. Heat 1 tablespoon olive oil and 15 g (½ oz) butter in a nonstick frying pan. Add the potato cakes and cook for 3–5 minutes on each side until golden and cooked through. Spoon 1 teaspoon crème fraîche on to each rosti, top with a large flake of smoked trout and scatter over some finely chopped dill to serve. **Total cooking time 25 minutes.**

crispy cod goujons

Serves **4**
Total cooking time **20 minutes**

100 g (3½ oz) **plain flour**
450 g (14½ oz) **skinless cod fillet**, cut into strips
250 g (8 oz) **fresh white breadcrumbs**
finely grated rind of 2 **limes**
1 teaspoon **black peppercorns**, crushed
2 **eggs**
150 ml (¼ pint) **vegetable oil**
salt and **pepper**
lime wedges, to serve

Lime & caper mayonnaise
200 ml (7 fl oz) **crème fraîche**
6 tablespoons **mayonnaise**
grated rind and juice of 1 **lime**
2 tablespoons **capers**, roughly chopped
3 tablespoons chopped **parsley**
1 tablespoon chopped **chives**

Place the flour on a plate and season generously with salt and pepper. Toss the fish strips in the seasoned flour and set aside.

Place the breadcrumbs on a separate plate and toss with the lime rind and crushed peppercorns. Beat the eggs thoroughly in a shallow bowl.

Heat the oil in a large, heavy-based frying pan. Dip each floured goujon in the egg and then in the breadcrumbs, working swiftly until they are all crumbed. Cook in 2 batches over a high heat for 3–4 minutes, turning once, until cooked through. Remove with a slotted spoon and drain on kitchen paper.

Meanwhile, for the mayonnaise, mix together the crème fraîche and mayonnaise, then stir in the remaining ingredients and season with pepper.

Place the mayonnaise in a small serving bowl and serve with the hot goujons, with lime wedges.

For pan-fried cod with lime & caper mayonnaise, toss 4 cod loin steaks, about 175 g (6 oz) each, in 50 g (2 oz) plain flour well seasoned with salt and pepper. Heat 4 tablespoons olive oil in a large, heavy-based frying pan and cook over a medium-high heat for 2–3 minutes on each side until golden and cooked through. Meanwhile, make the lime and caper mayonnaise as above. Serve the hot cod steaks with the creamy mayonnaise spooned over. **Total cooking time 10 minutes.**

smoked mackerel potato salad

Serves **4**

Total cooking time **20 minutes**

750 g (1½ lb) **new potatoes**, halved if large

200 g (7 oz) **crème fraîche**

2 teaspoons **creamed horseradish**

juice of **1 lemon**

2 tablespoons **pumpkin seeds**

4 **smoked mackerel fillets**, about 100 g (3½ oz) each, skinned and flaked

175 g (6 oz) **watercress**

salt and **pepper**

Cook the potatoes in a saucepan of boiling water for 15–16 minutes until tender.

Meanwhile, mix together the crème fraîche, horseradish and lemon juice in a large serving bowl and season to taste with salt and pepper.

Heat a nonstick frying pan over a medium-low heat and dry-fry the pumpkin seeds for 2–3 minutes, stirring frequently, until golden brown and toasted. Set aside.

Drain the potatoes, then refresh under cold running water and drain again. Mix with the crème fraîche mixture. Gently toss in the mackerel and watercress.

Serve sprinkled with the toasted pumpkin seeds.

For smoked mackerel dip, skin and flake 500 g (1 lb) smoked mackerel fillets into a bowl. Mix in 6–7 chopped spring onions, 275 g (9 oz) crème fraîche, the juice of ½ lemon and 2–3 teaspoons creamed horseradish. Season to taste with salt and pepper and serve with vegetable crudités and toasted pitta breads. **Total cooking time 10 minutes.**

spicy prawn & tomato curry

Serves **4**

Total cooking time **20 minutes**

2 tablespoons **hot curry powder**

1 teaspoon **ground turmeric**

4 **garlic cloves**, crushed

2 teaspoons peeled and finely grated **fresh root ginger**

2 tablespoons **ground cumin**

6 tablespoons **tomato purée**

1 teaspoon **caster sugar** or **grated palm sugar**

400 ml (14 fl oz) **water**

2 teaspoons **tamarind paste**

300 ml (½ pint) **coconut milk**

875 g (1½ lb) **raw tiger prawns**, peeled and deveined, with tails left on

200 g (7 oz) **cherry tomatoes**

salt and **pepper**

chopped **fresh coriander leaves**, to garnish

warmed **naan bread**, to serve

Put the curry powder, turmeric, garlic, ginger, cumin, tomato purée, sugar and measurement water in a heavy-based saucepan and mix together. Place over a high heat and bring to the boil. Cover, reduce the heat to low and simmer gently for 8–10 minutes.

Increase the heat to high, stir in the tamarind paste and coconut milk and bring back to the boil. Add the prawns and cherry tomatoes and cook, uncovered, for 4–5 minutes or until the prawns turn pink and are completely cooked through. Season well.

Ladle into warmed bowls, scatter with chopped coriander leaves and serve with warm naan bread.

For spicy prawn & tomato salad, arrange 500 g (1 lb) cooked peeled prawns, 4 sliced tomatoes and the leaves of 2 Baby Gem lettuces in a large salad bowl. Mix together 1 tablespoon medium curry powder, 6 tablespoons mayonnaise, the juice of 1 lemon and 5 tablespoons natural yogurt in a bowl, then season. Drizzle the dressing over the salad, toss to mix well and serve with crusty bread or warmed naan bread. **Total cooking time 10 minutes.**

frying-pan pizza with anchovies

Serves **4**

Total cooking time **25 minutes**

300 g (10 oz) **self-raising flour**, plus extra for dusting

1 teaspoon **dried thyme**

150 ml (¼ pint) warm **water**

1½ tablespoons **olive oil**

6 tablespoons **ready-made tomato pizza** or **pasta sauce**

50 g (2 oz) can **anchovies**, drained

2 tablespoons **capers**, rinsed and drained

125 g (4 oz) **mozzarella cheese**, diced

salt and **pepper**

Mix the flour in a bowl with the thyme and a generous pinch of salt and pepper. Pour in the measurement of warm water and olive oil, and mix to form a soft dough.

Divide the dough in half and roll out on a lightly floured surface to fit 2 large nonstick frying pans, approximately 28 cm (11 inches) across. Dust with a little flour. Heat the frying pans over a medium heat and lower the circles of dough carefully into the pans. Cook for about 10 minutes, turning once, until lightly golden.

Spread the sauce over the pizza bases and scatter with the anchovies and capers. Sprinkle over the mozzarella and cook under a preheated hot grill for 3–5 minutes until golden and bubbling. Serve immediately.

For mini tuna & anchovy pizzas, make the dough following the recipe above, then divide into approximately 16 small balls. Roll out each ball thinly and arrange on 2 lightly floured baking sheets. Cook in a preheated oven, 200°C (400°F), Gas Mark 6, for 3–4 minutes until lightly golden. Spread 6 tablespoons ready-made tomato pizza or pasta sauce on the mini pizzas, then drain a 200 g (7 oz) can tuna and divide between them. Top each one with 1 chopped anchovy fillet and a little mozzarella, then return to the oven for 8–10 minutes until the pizzas are crisp and melting. Serve hot with a lamb's lettuce salad. **Total cooking time 30 minutes.**

smoked haddock & spinach tart

Serves **4**

Total cooking time **30 minutes**

375 g (12 oz) **skinless
  smoked haddock fillet**
150 g (5 oz) **frozen leaf
  spinach**
125 ml (4 fl oz) **crème fraîche**
3 **eggs**, beaten
2 **spring onions**, sliced
375 g (12 oz) **ready-rolled
  puff pastry**
salt and **pepper**

Put the haddock in a pan, cover with boiling water and simmer for 3 minutes. Remove the fish from the pan and flake. Pour boiling water over the spinach until wilted, then squeeze away all the excess water.

Mix together the crème fraîche, beaten eggs (reserving 1 tablespoon) and spring onions and season well. Mix half this mixture with the spinach. Unwrap the pastry on to a baking sheet. Score a 1 cm (½ inch) border around the edges with a sharp knife and brush the border with the reserved egg.

Spoon the spinach mixture into the centre of the tart and scatter the haddock on top. Spoon over the remaining crème fraîche mixture and bake in a preheated oven, 200°C (400°F), Gas Mark 6, for 20 minutes or until golden and cooked through.

For smoked haddock & spinach gnocchi, place 300 g (10 oz) skinless smoked haddock fillet in a pan, cover with boiling water and simmer for 5 minutes until just cooked through, then remove and break into large flakes. Heat a large saucepan of lightly salted boiling water and cook 500 g (1 lb) fresh gnocchi according to the pack instructions. Add 150 g (5 oz) baby spinach leaves, drain and return to the pan. Add the haddock along with 75 ml (3 fl oz) crème fraîche and 1 teaspoon wholegrain mustard. Stir to coat and serve. **Total cooking time 15 minutes.**

creamy haddock gratin

Serves **4**
Total cooking time **30 minutes**

625 g (1¼ lb) **skinless
  haddock fillet**
600 ml (1 pint) **milk**
1 **bay leaf**
40 g (1½ oz) **butter**
40 g (1½ oz) **plain flour**
50 g (2 oz) **Gruyère cheese**,
  grated
½ teaspoon **prepared
  English mustard**

Topping
100 g (3½ oz) **fresh white
  breadcrumbs**
25 g (1 oz) **Gruyère cheese**,
  finely grated
finely grated rind of 1 **lemon**
2 tablespoons chopped
  parsley

To serve
salad leaves
lemon wedges

Place the haddock in a saucepan with the milk and bay leaf, bring to the boil and continue boiling for 3 minutes. Remove the fish with a slotted spoon, reserving the milk (discard the bay leaf), and divide between 4 individual gratin dishes.

Melt the butter in a separate saucepan, add the flour and cook over a medium heat, stirring, for a few seconds. Remove from the heat and add the reserved milk, a little at a time, stirring well between each addition. Return to the heat, then bring to the boil, stirring constantly, cooking until thickened. Remove from the heat and add the grated Gruyère and mustard.

Pour the sauce over the fish, dividing it evenly between the dishes. Mix together the ingredients for the topping and scatter over the sauce. Place on the top shelf of a preheated oven, 220°C (425°F), Gas Mark 7, for 10 minutes until the topping is golden and the sauce bubbling. Serve with a simple salad. and lemon wedges.

For haddock ceviche, chop 250 g (8 oz) very fresh skinless haddock fillet as finely as you can and place in a wide, shallow non-metallic dish. Sprinkle with 1 teaspoon sea salt, ½ teaspoon dried oregano and 75 ml (3 fl oz) lime juice. Cover and leave to marinate for 8 minutes. Drain the fish, discarding the white milky liquid. Add 3 chopped spring onions, 1 chopped green chilli and 4 tablespoons chopped fresh coriander. Serve spoonfuls of the ceviche on pieces of toasted baguette. **Total cooking time 10 minutes.**

keralan fish curry

Serves **4**

Total cooking time **25 minutes**

1 **red chilli**, deseeded and
  chopped
1 teaspoon **rapeseed oil**
1 teaspoon **ground coriander**
½ teaspoon **ground cumin**
½ teaspoon **ground turmeric**
4 **garlic cloves**
2.5 cm (1 inch) piece of **fresh
  root ginger**, peeled and
  chopped
1 tablespoon **coconut oil**
¼ teaspoon **fenugreek seeds**
2 **onions**, finely sliced
125 ml (4 fl oz) **coconut milk**
300 ml (½ pint) **water**
400 g (13 oz) **fresh mackerel
  fillets**, skinned and cut into
  5 cm (2 inch) pieces
salt and **pepper**

Place the chilli, rapeseed oil, coriander, cumin, turmeric, garlic and ginger in a mini food processor or small blender and blend to form a paste.

Heat the coconut oil in a wok or large frying pan, add the paste and fenugreek seeds and fry for 2–3 minutes. Add the onions, coconut milk and measurement water, season and bring to the boil, then cook for about 5 minutes until reduced.

Add the mackerel and simmer gently for 5–8 minutes or until cooked through.

For curried fish kebabs, mix together 3 tablespoons natural yogurt, 1 teaspoon each chopped garlic and fresh root ginger paste, the juice of ½ lime, 2 tablespoons curry paste and ½ teaspoon clear honey in a non-metallic bowl. Toss in 400 g (13 oz) chopped skinless salmon fillet and leave to marinate for 2–3 minutes. Thread the fish on to metal skewers, then cook on a hot barbecue or under a preheated hot grill for 2–3 minutes on each side or until cooked through. Serve with a crisp green salad. **Total cooking time 15 minutes.**

honey & chilli salmon skewers

Serves **4**

Total cooking time **30 minutes**

4 tablespoons **sweet chilli sauce**
4 tablespoons **clear honey**
4 tablespoons chopped **fresh coriander**
2 **spring onions**, finely sliced
1 tablespoon **sesame oil**
500 g (1 lb) **skinless salmon fillet**, cut into chunks
salt and **pepper**

Vegetable rice
250 g (8 oz) **easy-cook basmati rice**
2 tablespoons **sesame oil**
1 **red onion**, thinly sliced
6 **spring onions**, roughly chopped
175 g (6 oz) **sugar snap peas**, shredded
4 tablespoons chopped **fresh coriander**

Bring a saucepan of salted water to the boil and cook the rice for 15 minutes until just tender, then drain. Keep warm.

Meanwhile, mix together the chilli sauce, honey, coriander, spring onions and oil in a large bowl. Add the salmon chunks and toss well to coat. Season with a little pepper.

Thread the salmon on to 8 metal skewers. Place on a foil-lined grill rack and cook under a preheated medium grill for 7–8 minutes, turning 2–3 times, until lightly charred in places and cooked through.

Heat the oil for the vegetable rice in a large wok or heavy-based frying pan and stir-fry the red onion over a high heat for 3 minutes. Add the spring onions and sugar snap peas and stir-fry for a further 2 minutes until just beginning to soften. Add the drained rice and stir-fry for 2 minutes, then add the coriander and toss well. Spoon the rice on to serving plates and arrange the hot salmon skewers on top.

For honey & mustard salmon with courgette ribbons
, in a bowl, mix together 1 tablespoon each wholegrain mustard and light soy sauce, the juice of 1 lemon and 1 teaspoon clear honey. Place 4 salmon fillets on a foil-lined grill rack and brush over the honey mixture. Cook the salmon under a preheated medium-high grill for 8 minutes or until browned and cooked through. Remove and serve with steamed courgette ribbons and lemon wedges for squeezing over.
Total cooking time 10 minutes.

sea bass fillets with lentil salad

Serves **4**

Total cooking time **15 minutes**

4 tablespoons **olive oil**

400 g (13 oz) can **lentils**, drained

2 tablespoons chopped **parsley**

1 **red pepper**, cored, deseeded and diced

3 **spring onions**, sliced

1 **pink grapefruit**

4 **sea bass fillets**, about 150 g (5 oz) each

Heat 2 tablespoons of the olive oil in a small saucepan over a medium heat. Add the lentils, parsley, red pepper and spring onions and cook for 2–3 minutes.

Cut the peel from the grapefruit using a sharp knife, then divide into segments by cutting between the membranes, holding it over the pan to catch the juice. Mix the segments into the lentils.

Heat the remaining olive oil in a frying pan and fry the sea bass fillets for 2–3 minutes on each side until cooked through.

Serve on a bed of the lentils.

For sea bass fillets with crushed olive potatoes, cook 550 g (1 lb 2 oz) chopped new potatoes in a saucepan of boiling water for about 10 minutes until tender. Meanwhile, heat 2 tablespoons olive oil in a frying pan and cook 4 sea bass fillets, about 150 g (5 oz) each, skin side down first, for 3–4 minutes on each side until cooked through. Drain the potatoes, add 100 g (3½ oz) halved cherry tomatoes, 100 g (3½ oz) chopped pitted black olives, 3 tablespoons olive oil and 1 tablespoon chopped parsley and crush everything together with a fork. Divide the potatoes between 4 plates and top each one with a sea bass fillet. Total cooking time 20 minutes.

steamed spicy sea bream

Serves **2**

Total cooking time **20 minutes**

1 cm (½ inch) piece of **fresh root ginger**

2 **lemon grass stalks**, finely chopped

1 **garlic clove**, sliced

½ **red chilli**, finely chopped

1 **kaffir lime leaf**, finely sliced

handful of **fresh coriander**, chopped

3 tablespoons **fish sauce**

1 tablespoon **vegetable oil**, plus extra for oiling

2 **sea bream fillets**, about 150 g (5 oz) each

plain rice, to serve

Peel the ginger and cut into matchsticks. Mix with the lemon grass, garlic, chilli, lime leaf, coriander, fish sauce and oil.

Lay each fish fillet on a lightly oiled piece of foil, skin side down. Pour over the dressing. Fold the foil over tightly to seal, leaving a little air around the fish.

Place the foil packets in a steamer set over simmering water. Cook for 10–15 minutes until the fish is just cooked through. Serve with plain rice.

For mussels with Asian flavours, scrub 500 g (1 lb) live mussels and pull off any beards, discarding any mussels that refuse to close when tapped. Heat 1 tablespoon vegetable oil in a large saucepan. Cook 2 finely chopped lemon grass stalks, 1 cm (½ inch) piece of fresh root ginger, peeled and cut into matchsticks, 1 sliced garlic clove and ½ finely chopped red chilli for 30 seconds. Add 3 tablespoons fish sauce, 50 ml (2 fl oz) coconut milk and the cleaned mussels. Cover and cook for about 5 minutes until the mussels have opened. Discard any that remain closed. Toss in 300 g (10 oz) straight-to-wok rice noodles, heat through and serve scattered with chopped fresh coriander. **Total cooking time 25 minutes.**

japanese tuna soba noodles

Serves **2**

Total cooking time **10 minutes**

200 g (7 oz) **dried soba
  noodles**
1 tablespoon **vegetable oil**
2 **tuna steaks**, about 125 g
  (4 oz) each
¼ **cucumber**, sliced
2 **spring onions**, sliced
2 tablespoons **soy sauce**
2 tablespoons **mirin**
juice of ½ **lime**
2 teaspoons **caster sugar**
salt and **pepper**
sesame seeds, to serve

Cook the noodles according to the pack instructions. Meanwhile, heat a griddle pan until smoking hot. Rub the oil over the tuna steaks and season well. Cook on the pan for 1–2 minutes on each side or until charred on the outside but still rare inside.

Drain the noodles, cool under cold running water and drain again, then divide between serving bowls.

Cut the tuna into slices and toss together with the cucumber and spring onions. Mix together the soy sauce, mirin, lime juice and sugar until the sugar has dissolved. Pour over the noodles and sprinkle with sesame seeds to serve.

For sesame tuna with noodles, cook 200 g (7 oz) dried udon noodles according to the pack instructions. Drain. Heat 1 tablespoon vegetable oil in a wok. Add 2 sliced spring onions and 1 sliced garlic clove. Stir-fry briefly. Add 75 g (3 oz) halved shiitake mushrooms and 75 g (3 oz) sugar snap peas. Stir-fry for 2 minutes. Add 2 tablespoons each soy sauce and mirin, a pinch of caster sugar and the noodles. Cook for 2 minutes. Meanwhile, press 25 g (1 oz) sesame seeds over 2 tuna steaks, about 125 g (4 oz) each. Cook on a smoking hot griddle pan for 1–2 minutes on each side, then serve immediately with the noodles. **Total cooking time 20 minutes.**

smoked trout & rice noodle salad

Serves **4**

Total cooking time **10 minutes**

3 tablespoons **vegetable** or
groundnut oil

1 teaspoon **fish sauce**

1 tablespoon **lime juice**

1 tablespoon **light soy sauce**

375 g (12 oz) **cold cooked
rice noodles**

200 g (7 oz) **smoked trout
trimmings**, cut into strips

1 bunch of **fresh coriander**,
chopped

1 **red chilli**, deseeded and
chopped

1 small **cucumber**, finely
sliced

1 **red pepper**, cored,
deseeded and finely sliced

Combine the oil, fish sauce, lime juice and soy sauce
in a jar with a tight-fitting lid, and shake well to combine.

Place the noodles in a large bowl with the remaining
ingredients and toss with the dressing. Heap into 4 deep
bowls and serve.

For hot & sour noodle soup with crispy trout,

heat 1.2 litres (2 pints) stock in a saucepan with
3 tablespoons fish sauce, 1 tablespoon rice vinegar,
1 tablespoon lime juice and 1 tablespoon soft dark-
brown sugar. Add 1 deseeded and chopped red chilli,
1 tablespoon peeled and chopped fresh root ginger
and 1 sliced garlic clove. Simmer for 12–15 minutes.
Meanwhile, heat 1 tablespoon sesame oil in a frying
pan and cook 4 trout fillets, about 125 g (4 oz) each,
skin side down, for 7–8 minutes. Turn and cook for
a further 1–2 minutes. Divide 375 g (12 oz) cold
cooked rice noodles between 4 bowls and pour over
the broth. Top each with a fish fillet and serve scattered
with chopped fresh coriander. **Total cooking time
20 minutes.**

tomato & fennel fish pie

Serves **4**

Total cooking time **25 minutes**

4 tablespoons **olive oil**

1 **fennel bulb**, trimmed and chopped

2 **garlic cloves**, sliced

200 g (7 oz) **cherry tomatoes**

1 tablespoon **tomato purée**

50 ml (2 fl oz) **dry white wine**

75 ml (3 fl oz) **water**

300 g (10 oz) **skinless cod fillet**, cut into chunks

150 g (5 oz) large **raw peeled prawns**

750 g (1½ lb) **potatoes**, peeled and cut into chunks

2 **spring onions**, sliced

salt and **pepper**

Heat 1 tablespoon of the oil in a saucepan. Add the fennel and garlic and cook for 5–7 minutes until softened. Add the tomatoes and tomato purée and cook for a further 2 minutes until softened. Pour over the wine and cook until nearly boiled away, then add the measurement water and fish. Cook for 3 minutes. Add the prawns and cook for 3–5 minutes until just cooked through.

Meanwhile, cook the potatoes in a saucepan of salted boiling water for 12–15 minutes until soft. Drain and mash with the remaining oil, the spring onions and a little water to loosen. Season well with salt and pepper.

Arrange the fish and sauce in a baking dish. Spoon over the mash. Cook under a preheated hot grill for 3 minutes until browned. Serve immediately.

For prawns with tomato & fennel mayo, arrange 325 g (11 oz) large cooked peeled prawns on a plate. Mix together 3 tablespoons mayonnaise, 3 tablespoons fromage frais, 2 finely chopped sun-dried tomatoes, 1 teaspoon crushed fennel seeds and a squeeze of lemon juice. Serve with the prawns, a crisp green salad and some crusty brown bread. **Total cooking time 10 minutes.**

lemon & tomato swordfish kebabs

Serves **4**

Total cooking time **15 minutes**

350 g (11½ oz) **swordfish**,
   cut into 3 cm (1¼ inch)
   chunks
1 tablespoon **olive oil**
1 **lemon**, sliced
handful of **fresh bay leaves**
12 **cherry tomatoes**
salt and **pepper**
mixed green salad, to serve

Toss the fish in the oil to coat, then season with salt and pepper. Chop the lemon slices in half.

Heat a griddle pan until smoking hot. Thread the fish chunks on to metal skewers, alternating with the lemon slices, bay leaves and tomatoes.

Cook the kebabs on the griddle pan over a high heat for 4 minutes on each side or until the fish is cooked through. Serve with a mixed green salad.

For lemony swordfish with tomato sauce, place 4 swordfish steaks, about 175 g (6 oz) each, on a plate, cover with a mixture of 1 tablespoon olive oil, the finely grated rind and juice of 1 lemon and a handful of oregano, chopped, and leave to marinate. Meanwhile, heat 1 tablespoon olive oil in a frying pan. Add 2 quartered red peppers, cored and deseeded, 1 teaspoon caster sugar and 1 tablespoon white wine vinegar and leave to gently cook for 10 minutes. Add 200 g (7 oz) cherry tomatoes and cook for a further 10–15 minutes until the vegetables are very soft. Season well. While the vegetables finish cooking, cook the swordfish under a preheated hot grill for 7 minutes on each side. Serve alongside the peppers and tomatoes. **Total cooking time 30 minutes.**

seafood risotto

Serves **6**

Total cooking time **30 minutes**

250 g (8 oz) **mixed fish fillets**, such as sea bass, monkfish and red mullet, cut into 2.5 cm (1 inch) chunks

200 g (7 oz) small **raw prawns, shells on**

1.5 litres (2½ pints) **fish stock**

150 ml (¼ pint) **dry white wine**

1 tablespoon **olive oil**

25 g (1 oz) **butter**

1 small **onion**, finely chopped

½ **fennel bulb**, trimmed and finely chopped

500 g (1 lb) **risotto rice**

250 g (8 oz) **cleaned live clams**

100 g (3½ oz) **raw squid rings**

lemon juice, to taste

salt and **pepper**

Place the fish and prawns in a large saucepan. Pour over the stock and wine and bring to the boil. Cook for 1–2 minutes until the seafood just turns opaque. Remove the seafood from the pan and set aside. Keep the stock simmering.

Heat the oil with a little of the butter in a large saucepan. Add the onion and fennel and cook for 5 minutes. Stir in the rice until well coated. Add the hot stock, a ladleful at a time, stirring and simmering after each addition until the stock is absorbed before adding the next. After 15 minutes when the stock is absorbed and the rice is nearly cooked through, add the clams and cook for 3 minutes, then add the cooked seafood, squid rings and remaining butter. Season and squeeze over lemon juice to taste.

Cover and leave to stand for 2 minutes. Discard any clams that remain closed, then serve.

For seafood noodle broth, heat 1. 5 litres (2½ pints) fish stock, 2 peeled slices of fresh root ginger and 1 lemon grass stalk. Add 250 g (8 oz) cleaned live clams, 100 g (3½ oz) raw peeled prawns and 200 g (7 oz) dried fine rice noodles. Cook for 3 minutes. Add 75 g (3 oz) raw squid rings. Cook for 2 minutes or until all the seafood is cooked. Discard any clams that remain closed. Add some chopped fresh coriander, then serve. **Total cooking time 10 minutes.**

lemony tuna & borlotti bean salad

Serves **4**
Total cooking time **10 minutes**

grated rind and juice of
  1 lemon
3 tablespoons **olive oil**
2 **spring onions**, finely sliced
2 x 175 g (6 oz) cans **tuna in
  oil** or **spring water**, drained
  and flaked
2 x 400 g (13 oz) cans **borlotti
  beans**, rinsed and drained
1 small bunch of **flat leaf
  parsley**, roughly chopped
75 g (3 oz) **rocket** or **rocket**
  and **watercress**
salt and **pepper**

Combine the lemon rind and juice and olive oil in a jug
and season with salt and pepper.

Mix all of the remaining ingredients gently together and
spoon into 4 shallow bowls. Drizzle with the dressing
and serve immediately.

For seared tuna with warm borlotti beans, heat
2 tablespoons olive oil in a frying pan and cook
1 chopped red onion for 7–8 minutes. Add 2 x 400 g
(13 oz) cans borlotti beans, rinsed and drained,
1 bunch of flat leaf parsley, chopped, and 125 ml
(4 fl oz) vegetable stock. Season and simmer for
7–8 minutes. Meanwhile, rub 1 tablespoon olive oil
over 4 small fresh tuna steaks and season. Heat a
griddle pan until smoking hot and cook the tuna for
3–4 minutes, turning once, until seared outside but
pink inside. Set aside. Spoon the beans on to 4 warmed
plates and top each with a seared tuna steak. Garnish
with a few rocket leaves and squeeze over the juice of
1 lemon to serve. **Total cooking time 25 minutes**

vegetarian

cherry tomato & goats' cheese tart

Serves **4**

Total cooking time **30 minutes**

375 g (12 oz) **ready-rolled puff pastry**
plain flour, for dusting
8 tablespoons **chilli jam**
400 g (13 oz) **mixed red** and **yellow cherry tomatoes**, halved
200 g (7 oz) **soft goats' cheese**
4 tablespoons roughly chopped **mint leaves**, to garnish
rocket salad, to serve (optional)

Unroll the puff pastry on to a lightly floured work surface and cut into a 30 x 20 cm (12 x 8 inch) rectangle. Using a sharp knife, score a border 1.5 cm (¾ inch) from the edge of the pastry. Put the pastry on a baking sheet and place in a preheated oven, 220°C (425°F), Gas Mark 7, for 10–12 minutes or until the pastry has risen and is cooked through and lightly golden. Cool for 5 minutes.

Spoon the chilli jam evenly over the base of the puff pastry case, then top with the tomatoes. Crumble over the goats' cheese and return the filled tart to the oven for 6–8 minutes or until the cheese has melted and the tart has heated through.

Scatter over the chopped mint and serve with a rocket salad, if liked.

For chilli, cherry tomato & goats' cheese salad, halve 500 g (1 lb) mixed red and yellow cherry tomatoes and put in a large serving dish, then crumble over 200 g (7 oz) soft goats' cheese. Mix together 6 tablespoons extra virgin olive oil, 1 deseeded and finely chopped red chilli, 3 tablespoons red wine vinegar, 1 teaspoon clear honey and 1 teaspoon Dijon mustard in a bowl, then season. Drizzle the dressing over the tomato and goats' cheese. Scatter over a small handful of mint leaves and serve. **Total cooking time 10 minutes.**

pepper & artichoke paella

Serves **4**
Total cooking time **30 minutes**

2 tablespoons **olive oil**
1 **onion**, finely chopped
2 **garlic cloves**, chopped
250 g (8 oz) **paella rice**
1 teaspoon **sweet smoked paprika**
pinch of **dried chilli flakes**
pinch of **saffron threads**
125 ml (4 fl oz) **dry white wine**
400 g (13 oz) can **cherry tomatoes**
300 ml (½ pint) **vegetable stock**
125 g (4 oz) **green beans**, topped and tailed and halved
2 **roasted red peppers** from a jar, drained and cut into strips
4 **roasted artichoke hearts** from a jar, drained and quartered
handful of **parsley**, chopped
salt and **pepper**
lemon wedges, to serve

Heat the oil in a deep frying pan or paella dish, add the onion and cook for 5 minutes until softened. Stir in the garlic and cook for 1 minute more. Add the rice and spices and stir around the pan until well coated. Pour over the wine and cook until bubbled away.

Add the cherry tomatoes followed by the vegetable stock. Cover and leave to simmer for 10 minutes.

Meanwhile, cook the beans in a saucepan of boiling water for 2 minutes until starting to soften.

Add to the paella along with the peppers and artichokes and cook for 5 minutes more until the rice is soft. Season to taste, scatter over the parsley and serve with lemon wedges.

For artichoke crostini with peppers, drain a 400 g (13 oz) can artichoke hearts and pulse in a food processor. Add 3 tablespoons olive oil, 3 tablespoons crème fraîche and 1 tablespoon lemon juice. Season and pulse until almost smooth. Slice a ciabatta loaf and drizzle with olive oil. Toast under a preheated hot grill for 2–3 minutes on each side, then rub with a garlic clove. Spread with the artichoke purée and top with roasted red peppers from a jar and rocket leaves. Total cooking time **10 minutes**.

cheese & onion rarebit

Serves **4**
Total cooking time **10 minutes**

6 tablespoons **caramelized
    onion** or **onion chutney**
4 large slices of **sourdough
    bread**, lightly toasted
150 g (5 oz) **ready-made
    four-cheese sauce**
150 g (5 oz) **mature Cheddar
    cheese**, grated
2 tablespoons **wholegrain
    mustard**
2 **egg yolks**
salt and **pepper**

To serve
Worcestershire sauce
    (optional)
green salad

Spread the chutney over the toasted bread.

Put all the remaining ingredients into a bowl and beat
together. Season to taste and spread over the toasts.

Place under a preheated medium-hot grill for 4–6
minutes or until the topping is melting and golden.
Serve sprinkled with Worcestershire sauce, if liked,
and a green salad.

For cheese & onion pizza, mix 1 tablespoon
wholegrain mustard with 150 g (5 oz) ready-made
four-cheese sauce and 2 tablespoons caramelized
onion chutney. Spread thinly over 2 large, ready-made
pizza bases placed on 2 baking sheets. Top with
1 small, thinly sliced red onion and 75 g (3 oz) pitted
black olives. Place in a preheated oven, 200°C (400°F),
Gas Mark 6, for 12–15 minutes until crisp. Serve with
a salad, as above. **Total cooking time 20 minutes.**

aubergine parmigiana

Serves **4**

Total cooking time **30 minutes**

3 tablespoons **olive oil**

2 **aubergines**, trimmed and sliced

1 **onion**, diced

2 **garlic cloves**, crushed

400 g (13 oz) can **chopped tomatoes**

1 teaspoon chopped **oregano**

200 g (7 oz) **mozzarella cheese**, grated

2 **beef tomatoes**, thinly sliced

6 tablespoons grated **Parmesan cheese**

Heat 2 tablespoons of the olive oil in a frying pan and cook the aubergine slices in batches until golden.

Add the remaining oil to a saucepan and sauté the onion and garlic for 3–4 minutes. Stir in the canned tomatoes and oregano.

Layer the aubergine slices in a large ovenproof dish with the mozzarella and beef tomatoes.

Pour over the tomato sauce and sprinkle with the grated Parmesan. Bake in a preheated oven, 200°C (400°F), Gas Mark 6, for 15–18 minutes. Serve warm.

For ricotta-stuffed aubergine rolls, heat a griddle pan. When smoking hot, griddle slices of aubergine that have been cut lengthways from 2 aubergines, for 2–3 minutes on each side until golden. Mix together 150 g (5 oz) ricotta cheese, 150 g (5 oz) chopped mozzarella cheese, 2 teaspoons chopped basil leaves and 2 sliced spring onions. Place 1 teaspoon of the ricotta mixture on to the end of each slice of aubergine, then roll up each slice and place seam side down in an ovenproof dish. Pour over 300 g (10 oz) ready-made tomato pasta sauce and bake in a preheated oven, 190°C (375°F), Gas Mark 5, for 12–15 minutes until the cheese starts to melt. Serve with a rocket salad. **Total cooking time 25 minutes.**

courgette fritters & poached eggs

Serves **4**

Total cooking time **20 minutes**

4 **courgettes**, trimmed and grated
4 tablespoons **self-raising flour**
40 g (1½ oz) **Parmesan cheese**, grated
2 tablespoons **olive oil**
4 **eggs**
pepper

Place the grated courgette, flour and grated Parmesan in a bowl and mix together well.

Squeeze into walnut-sized balls and then gently flatten.

Heat the oil in a deep frying pan and, working in batches if necessary, fry the fritters for 2–3 minutes on each side until golden.

Meanwhile, bring a large saucepan of water to a gentle simmer and stir with a large spoon to create a swirl. Carefully break 2 eggs into the water and cook for 3 minutes. Remove with a slotted spoon and keep warm. Repeat with the remaining eggs.

Serve the fritters topped with the poached eggs and sprinkled with pepper.

For griddled courgettes with mint & lemon, use a vegetable peeler to slice 4 trimmed courgettes very thinly, brush each slice with olive oil and sprinkle with 2 crushed garlic cloves. Heat a griddle pan until smoking and cook the slices for 2–3 minutes on each side until charred (this can also be done on a hot barbecue grill). Place on a serving platter and scatter over the grated rind and juice of 1 lemon and 1 finely chopped green chilli. Toss gently. To serve, drizzle over 1 tablespoon olive oil and sprinkle with 2 tablespoons chopped mint leaves and 20 g (¾ oz) Parmesan shavings. **Total cooking time 10 minutes.**

tricolore pitta pizzas

Serves **4**

Total cooking time **10 minutes**

4 **pitta breads**

1 tablespoon **olive oil**

350 g (11½ oz) **spinach leaves**

4 tablespoons **tomato ketchup**

2 **yellow peppers**, cored, deseeded and finely sliced

250 g (8 oz) **roasted red peppers from a jar**, drained and sliced

250 g (8 oz) **mozzarella cheese**, grated

Cook the pitta breads under a preheated hot grill for 1–2 minutes. While they are still warm, run a knife down one side of each pitta bread and split it open to give 2 flat pieces of bread.

Meanwhile, heat the olive oil in a frying pan and add the spinach. Stir for 1–2 minutes until it starts to wilt.

Spread 1 tablespoon of the ketchup on each flatbread. Top with the spinach, sliced yellow and red peppers and finally the mozzarella.

Place under a preheated hot grill for 4–5 minutes until the cheese is melted and golden.

For tricolore pizzas, place 2 medium ready-made pizza bases on a large baking sheet and spread each one with 2 tablespoons passata. Top each one with 1 sliced tomato, ½ red and ½ yellow pepper, cored, deseeded and sliced, ¼ thinly sliced red onion and 50 g (2 oz) grated mozzarella cheese. Sprinkle with 6–8 shredded basil leaves and bake in a preheated oven, 200°C (400°F) Gas Mark 6, for 11–13 minutes. Cut into wedges and serve with a crisp green salad. **Total cooking time 20 minutes.**

saffron risotto

Serves **4**

Total cooking time **30 minutes**

2 tablespoons **olive oil**
1 **onion**, finely diced
300 g (10 oz) **risotto rice**
200 ml (7 fl oz) **white wine**
750 ml (1¼ pints) hot
  vegetable stock
large pinch of **saffron threads**
25 g (1 oz) **butter**
40 g (1½ oz) **Parmesan**
  cheese, grated

Heat the olive oil in a saucepan and sauté the onion for 3–5 minutes until softened.

Stir in the rice and continue to stir, until the edges of the grains look translucent. Pour in the wine and cook for 1–2 minutes until it is absorbed.

Add a ladle of the hot vegetable stock and the saffron and stir constantly until it has all been absorbed. Repeat with the remaining hot stock, adding a ladle at a time, until the rice is al dente.

Remove from the heat and stir in the butter and half the grated Parmesan.

Serve sprinkled with the remaining Parmesan.

For warm saffron rice salad, heat 2 tablespoons olive oil in a frying pan and cook 1 large chopped onion and 3 crushed garlic cloves for 4–5 minutes until golden. Stir in a 300 g (10 oz) pack ready-cooked long-grain rice and heat through until piping hot. Meanwhile, crumble 1 large pinch of saffron threads into a small saucepan, add 3 tablespoons hot vegetable stock and simmer for 1 minute until infused, then stir into the rice with 2 tablespoons sultanas, 3 tablespoons toasted flaked almonds, 2 tablespoons pitted green olives, 1 tablespoon chopped mint leaves and 2 tablespoons chopped parsley. **Total cooking time 10 minutes.**

cheesy tomato pasta bake

Serves **4**

Total cooking time **30 minutes**

2 tablespoons **olive oil**, plus
    extra for oiling

2 **garlic cloves**, finely chopped

400 g (13 oz) can **chopped
    tomatoes**

handful of **oregano leaves**,
    chopped, plus extra
    to garnish

400 g (13 oz) **dried penne**

250 g (8 oz) **mozzarella
    cheese**, cubed

50 g (2 oz) **Parmesan
    cheese**, grated

salt and **pepper**

Heat the oil in a large frying pan, add the garlic and cook for 30 seconds. Stir in the tomatoes and oregano and simmer, fairly vigorously, for 10–12 minutes or until thickened. Season well.

Meanwhile, cook the pasta in a large saucepan of salted boiling water according to the pack instructions until al dente. Drain, reserving a little of the cooking water, and return to the pan.

Stir in the tomato sauce, reserving 2 tablespoons of the sauce. Add a little cooking water to loosen if needed.

Spoon half the pasta into an oiled ovenproof dish. Cover with half the mozzarella and Parmesan, then add the remaining pasta. Spoon over the reserved tomato sauce and scatter with the remaining cheese.

Place in a preheated oven, 200°C (400°F), Gas Mark 6, for 15 minutes or until golden and bubbling. Scatter with oregano leaves to garnish and serve.

For simple cheese & tomato penne, cook and drain the penne as above. Stir through 4 chopped tomatoes, 3 tablespoons crème fraîche and a handful of chopped rocket leaves. Served topped with 150 g (5 oz) sliced mozzarella cheese and a little grated Parmesan cheese. **Total cooking time 10 minutes.**

mushroom-topped potato rösti

Serves **4**
Total cooking time **30 minutes**

3 **potatoes**, scrubbed but
   unpeeled, about 625 g
   (1¼ lb) total weight
½ **onion**, very thinly sliced
4 tablespoons **vegetable oil**,
   plua extra for oiling
50 g (2 oz) **butter**
1 **garlic clove**, chopped
250 g (8 oz) **button
   mushrooms**, thinly sliced
2 tablespoons finely chopped
   parsley (optional)
salt and **pepper**
1 large **bunch of watercress**,
   to serve

Cook the potatoes whole in a large saucepan of lightly salted boiling water for 8–10 minutes. Drain and set aside to cool slightly. Wearing rubber gloves to protect your hands from the heat, coarsely grate the potatoes and mix in a bowl with the sliced onion, 2 tablespoons of the oil and plenty of salt and pepper.

Heat the remaining oil in a large, nonstick frying pan and add the rosti mixture, pushing down to flatten it so that it covers the base of the pan. Cook for 7–8 minutes, then slide on to an oiled plate or board. Flip the rosti back into the pan to cook the other side for 7–8 minutes until crisp and golden.

Meanwhile, melt the butter in a frying pan and cook the garlic and mushrooms gently for 6–7 minutes until softened and golden. Season to taste with salt and pepper, then stir in the chopped parsley, if using.

Cut the rosti into wedges, then arrange on serving plates, scatter over the watercress and spoon over the warm mushrooms with their juices. Serve immediately.

For garlic mushrooms on toast, melt the butter and fry the garlic and mushrooms, following the recipe above. Heat a griddle pan and toast 4 large slices of sourdough or rustic-style bread until crisp and nicely charred. Top with the watercress, as above, and spoon over the hot garlic mushrooms. Serve immediately. **Total cooking time 10 minutes.**

cheesy polenta & mushrooms

Serves **4**

Total cooking time **25 minutes**

400 g (13 oz) **mixed wild mushrooms**, such as **porcini, girolles** and **chanterelles**
25 g (1 oz) **butter**
2 **garlic cloves**, chopped
5 **whole sage leaves**
50 ml (2 fl oz) **dry vermouth**
salt and **pepper**

Polenta
750 ml (1¼ pints) **water**
200 g (7 oz) **instant polenta**
50 g (2 oz) **Parmesan cheese**, freshly grated
50 g (2 oz) **butter**, cubed

Brush away any soil and grit from the mushrooms with a moist cloth, then slice the porcini and tear any other large mushrooms in half. Set aside.

Melt the butter in a large frying pan over a medium-high heat. Add the garlic, sage and the dense, tougher mushrooms and cook for 2–3 minutes. Add the remaining mushrooms, season with salt and pepper and cook for 2–3 minutes until soft and cooked through. Pour in the vermouth and cook, stirring, for 1 minute.

For the polenta, bring the measurement water to the boil in a large, heavy-based saucepan. Put the polenta in a jug and pour into the water in a slow but steady stream, stirring vigorously with a wooden spoon to prevent any lumps forming. Reduce the heat to a slow simmer and cook, stirring frequently, for about 5 minutes, or until the polenta is thick and comes away from the side of the pan. Stir in the butter and season with salt and pepper.

Divide the polenta between 4 serving plates, then top with the mushrooms.

For cheesy polenta with mushrooms & tomato, cook the mushrooms as above, but replace the rosemary with 3 chopped thyme sprigs and use 150 ml (¼ pint) full-bodied red wine instead of the vermouth. When the wine has boiled for 1 minute, stir in 300 ml (½ pint) passata. Season with salt and pepper and bring to the boil, then simmer for 5 minutes. Cook the polenta as above, then gradually stir in the cheese. Serve with the mushroom and tomato mixture. **Total cooking time 10 minutes.**

carrot & beetroot tabbouleh

Serves **4**

Total cooking time **10 minutes**

150 g (5 oz) **bulgar wheat**

1 **garlic clove**, crushed

pinch of **ground cinnamon**

pinch of **ground allspice**

2 tablespoons **pomegranate molasses**

5 tablespoons **extra virgin olive oil**

1 **carrot**, peeled and grated

125 g (4 oz) **ready-cooked beetroot**, cubed

2 **spring onions**, sliced

½ **green chilli**, chopped

large handful of **mint**, chopped

large handful of **parsley**, chopped

50 g (2 oz) **feta cheese**, crumbled

salt and **pepper**

Prepare the bulgar wheat according to the pack instructions, then drain thoroughly.

Mix together the garlic, spices, pomegranate molasses and olive oil. Toss together with the bulgar wheat, carrot, beetroot, spring onions, chilli, mint and parsley and season to taste. Scatter over the feta to serve.

For spicy carrot stew with couscous, heat

1 tablespoon olive oil in a saucepan and cook
1 sliced onion, 1 peeled and sliced parsnip and
2 peeled and sliced carrots in 1 tablespoon oil
for 7 minutes until softened. Stir in 2 teaspoons ras
el hanout spice mix and 2 crushed garlic cloves. Pour
over 300 ml (½ pint) vegetable stock and simmer
for 10 minutes. Add 200 g (7 oz) drained canned
chickpeas and a little lemon juice and heat through.
Meanwhile, pour 350 ml (12 fl oz) hot stock over
300 g (10 oz) couscous in a bowl, cover and leave
for 5-10 minutes until all the liquid is absorbed and the
couscous has swelled. Stir through 25 g (1 oz) toasted
flaked almonds, 1 sliced spring onion and a handful
each of chopped mint and parsley. Serve with the carrot
stew. **Total cooking time 25 minutes.**

spinach & pepper quesadillas

Serves **4**

Total cooking time **30 minutes**

300 g (10 oz) **baby spinach leaves**

200 g (7 oz) **roasted red peppers from a jar**, drained and roughly chopped

8 **spring onions**, finely chopped

200 g (7 oz) **smoked cheese**, finely diced

150 g (5 oz) **mild Cheddar cheese**, grated

1 **red chilli**, deseeded and finely chopped

4 tablespoons finely chopped **fresh coriander leaves**

8 **soft corn tortillas**

salt and **pepper**

olive oil, for oiling

soured cream, to serve

Blanch the spinach in a large saucepan of lightly salted boiling water for 1–2 minutes. Drain thoroughly through a fine sieve, pressing out all the liquid. Transfer to a bowl with the roasted peppers, spring onions, smoked cheese, Cheddar, chilli and coriander. Season and mix.

Scatter a quarter of the spinach mixture over a tortilla, top with another tortilla and press together. Make 3 more quesadillas in the same way.

Oil 2 large frying pans with a little olive oil and place over a medium heat. Put 1 quesadilla into each pan and cook for 2 minutes until golden. Invert on to a plate, then slide back into the pan and cook for another 2 minutes until the filling is hot and the cheese is just melting. Set aside while you cook the other 2.

Cut each quesadilla into 4 and serve with soured cream.

For pepper, spinach & egg noodle stir-fry, heat 3 tablespoons light olive oil in a large wok or frying pan, add 8 sliced spring onions, 2 crushed garlic cloves, 1 sliced red chilli, 400 g (13 oz) roasted red peppers from a jar, drained and sliced, and 300 g (10 oz) baby spinach leaves and stir-fry for 4–5 minutes over a high heat or until the spinach has just wilted. Stir in 400 g (13 oz) ready-cooked fresh egg noodles and 6 tablespoons sweet chilli sauce, and cook for 1–2 minutes or until piping hot. **Total cooking time 10 minutes.**

cauliflower cheese

Serves **4**
Total cooking time **10 minutes**

1 large **cauliflower**, broken
  into pieces
50 g (2 oz) **butter**
4 tablespoons **plain flour**
½ teaspoon **English mustard
  powder**
500 ml (17 fl oz) **milk**
100 g (3½ oz) **mature
  Cheddar cheese**, grated
2 tablespoons **pumpkin
  seeds**

Cook the cauliflower in a large saucepan of boiling water for 5–6 minutes until tender.

Meanwhile, melt the butter in a small saucepan, then stir in the flour and mustard powder to make a roux. Cook for 1–2 minutes, then gradually whisk in the milk and cook, stirring constantly, until the sauce is thick and smooth. Simmer for 1 minute, then stir in half the grated cheese.

Drain the cauliflower and place in an ovenproof dish. Pour over the cheese sauce, then sprinkle with the pumpkin seeds and remaining cheese. Cook under a preheated hot grill for 2–3 minutes until bubbling and golden.

For cauliflower cheese soup, melt 25 g (1 oz) butter in a saucepan, add 1 finely chopped onion and cook for 2–3 minutes. Add the florets of 1 large cauliflower, 1 peeled and chopped potato, 600 ml (1 pint) hot vegetable stock and 400 ml (14 fl oz) milk, season with salt and pepper and bring to the boil. Reduce the heat and simmer for 15–16 minutes until the vegetables are soft. Using a hand-held blender, blend the soup until smooth, adding a little more milk if needed. Sprinkle with 2 tablespoons grated mature Cheddar cheese. **Total cooking time 25 minutes.**

storecupboard spicy bean soup

Serves **4**

Total cooking time **30 minutes**

2 tablespoons **vegetable oil**

1 large **onion**, chopped

1 **red pepper**, cored, deseeded and chopped

2 **garlic cloves**, chopped

30 g (1¼ oz) **sachet Mexican fajita, taco** or **chilli con carne spice mix**

400 g (13 oz) can **red kidney beans**, rinsed and drained

400 g (13 oz) can **black beans**, drained and rinsed

400 g (13 oz) can **chopped tomatoes**

750 ml (1¼ pints) boiling **water**

1 **vegetable stock cube**, crumbled

To serve

4 tablespoons **soured cream**

25 g (1 oz) **tortilla chips** (optional)

Heat the vegetable oil in a large, heavy-based saucepan or flameproof casserole dish and cook the onion and pepper over a medium-high heat for 4 minutes. Add the garlic and fry for a further 2 minutes until lightly coloured.

Stir in the spice mix, then add half of the beans, the chopped tomatoes, measurement water and stock cube. Stir well, bring to the boil and simmer for 10–12 minutes until slightly thickened.

Use a hand-held blender to blend the soup until almost smooth, then stir in the remaining beans and heat through. Ladle into 4 deep bowls and serve immediately with a drizzle of soured cream and a scattering of tortilla chips, if liked.

For spicy bean tacos, heat 2 tablespoons vegetable oil in a large saucepan and cook 1 large chopped onion and 1 cored, deseeded and chopped red pepper and fry for 4 minutes. Add 2 garlic cloves, chopped, and fry for a further 2 minutes. Add a 30 g (1¼ oz) sachet Mexican fajita, taco, or chilli con carne spice mix, 400 g (13 oz) can each red kidney beans and black beans, rinsed and drained, 2 diced tomatoes and 75 ml (3 fl oz) water. Simmer for 2–3 minutes, then spoon into 8 warmed taco shells and serve immediately with 4 tablespoons soured cream. **Total cooking time 10 minutes.**

frying pan macaroni cheese

Serves **4**
Total cooking time **30 minutes**

325 g (11 oz) **dried macaroni**
50 g (2 oz) **butter**
50 g (2 oz) **plain flour**
600 ml (1 pint) **milk**
100 g (3½ oz) **Cheddar cheese**, grated
25 g (1 oz) **dried white breadcrumbs**
25 g (1 oz) **Parmesan cheese**, grated
salt and **pepper**

Cook the pasta in a large saucepan of salted boiling water according to the pack instructions until al dente.

Meanwhile, melt the butter in a large, ovenproof frying pan and stir in the flour to make a smooth paste. Cook until golden, then gradually whisk in the milk. Bring to the boil over a medium heat, then simmer for about 3 minutes until slightly thickened. Remove from the heat, stir in the cheese and season.

Drain the pasta, then tip into the frying pan. Stir into the cheese sauce until well combined. Scatter over the breadcrumbs and Parmesan.

Place in a preheated oven, 190°C (375°F), Gas Mark 5, for 15 minutes or until golden brown and bubbling.

For pasta in a cheesy sauce, cook 400 g (13 oz) dried chifferi pasta in a large saucepan of salted boiling water according to the pack instructions until al dente. Meanwhile, place 1 garlic clove and 100 ml (3½ fl oz) double cream in a saucepan and cook for 5 minutes. Remove and discard the garlic and stir in 50 g (2 oz) grated Parmesan cheese. Drain the pasta and return to the pan. Stir through the sauce and serve immediately. **Total cooking time 10 minutes.**

fiorentina pizzas

Serves **4**
Total cooking time **30 minutes**

2 large **ready-made pizza
 bases**
500 g (1 lb) **passata**
2 tablespoons **olive oil**
2 **garlic cloves**, sliced
1 **red onion**, sliced
500 g (1 lb) **spinach leaves**
4 **eggs**
2 tablespoons **pine nuts**
200 g (7 oz) **mozzarella
 cheese**, grated
pepper

Place the pizza bases on 2 baking sheets and spread
each one with the passata.

Heat the olive oil in a large frying pan and sauté the
garlic and onion for 2–3 minutes, then add the spinach
and stir until it has completely wilted.

Spread the wilted spinach over the pizza bases and
make 2 small hollows in each pizza topping. Break the
eggs into the hollows.

Sprinkle each pizza with the pine nuts ar d mozzarella
and season with pepper.

Bake in a preheated oven, 200°C (400°F), Gas Mark 6,
for 12–15 minutes until the eggs are co ɔked. Cut into
slices and serve immediately.

For healthy pitta pizzas, lightly poach 4 eggs.
Meanwhile, toast 4 wholemeal pitta breads under
a preheated hot grill for 1–2 minutes on each side,
then spread with 1 tablespoon tomato ketchup. Heat
1 tablespoon olive oil in a frying pan, add 400 g (13 oz)
spinach leaves and fry until wilted. Spread the spinach
over the toasted pitta breads. Top each one with a
poached egg, then sprinkle with 1 tablespoon each of
pine nuts and grated mozzarella cheese. Cook under
the hot grill for 3–4 minutes until the cheese melts.
Total cooking time 10 minutes.

spinach, pine nut & cheese filo pie

Serves **4**

Total cooking time **30 minutes**

1 tablespoon **olive oil**

1 **onion**, roughly chopped

1 **garlic clove**, thinly sliced

75 g (3 oz) **pine nuts**, toasted

1 kg (2 lb) **frozen leaf spinach**, defrosted and well drained

2 **eggs**, plus 2 **egg yolks**

2 x 200 g (7 oz) packs **feta cheese**, drained and crumbled

2 teaspoons **ground nutmeg**

6 sheets of **filo pastry**, defrosted if frozen

25 g (1 oz) **butter**, melted

25 g (1 oz) **Parmesan cheese**, grated

salt and **pepper**

salad leaves dressed with olive oil and lemon juice, to serve

Heat the oil in a large, heavy-based frying pan and cook the onion and garlic over a medium heat, stirring occasionally, for 5 minutes. Add the pine nuts and spinach and cook, stirring, for 3–4 minutes until heated through.

Remove the pan from the heat and tip the mixture into a bowl. Add the whole eggs, egg yolks, feta and nutmeg, stir well and season with a little salt and plenty of pepper. Transfer to a large gratin dish.

Crumple the sheets of filo pastry over the top, brush with the melted butter and scatter over the Parmesan. Place in a preheated oven, 180°C (350°F), Gas Mark 4, for 10–12 minutes until the pastry is golden and crisp.

Serve hot with salad leaves dressed with olive oil and lemon juice.

For spinach & cheese pesto pasta, bring a large saucepan of lightly salted water to the boil and cook 2 x 250 g (8 oz) packs fresh spinach and ricotta tortellini for 2–3 minutes, or according to the pack instructions, until just tender. Drain the pasta, return to the pan and stir in 4 tablespoons ready-made green pesto. Serve in warmed bowls, scattered with Parmesan cheese shavings. **Total cooking time 10 minutes.**

avocado, pepper & olive salad

Serves **4**

Total cooking time **10 minutes**

1 tablespoon **sesame seeds**

2 **avocados**, stoned, peeled
and chopped

juice of **1 lime**

1 **red pepper**, cored,
deseeded and chopped

1 **yellow pepper**, cored,
deseeded and chopped

½ **cucumber**, finely chopped

2 **carrots**, peeled and
chopped

2 **tomatoes**, chopped

4 **spring onions**, sliced

10 **pitted black olives**, halved

1 **Cos lettuce**, roughly torn

4 tablespoons **ready-made
salad dressing**

1 tablespoon chopped **mint**

Heat a nonstick frying pan over a medium-low heat
and dry-fry the sesame seeds for 2 minutes, stirring
frequently, until golden brown and toasted. Set aside.

Meanwhile, place the avocados in a large bowl and
toss with the lime juice to prevent discoloration. Gently
toss together with the remaining ingredients except
the sesame seeds.

Sprinkle the salad with the toasted sesame seeds
and serve.

For peperonata with avocado & olives, heat 3
tablespoons olive oil in a frying pan, add 2 sliced garlic
cloves and 3 sliced onions and cook for 1–2 minutes.
Core, deseed and slice 2 red peppers and 2 yellow
peppers, then add to the pan and cook for 10 minutes.
Add 350 g (11½ oz) chopped ripe tomatoes and
cook for a further 12–15 minutes until the peppers
are soft. Stir in 1 stoned, peeled and chopped avocado,
12 halved pitted black olives and a small handful of
basil leaves. Serve with crusty bread. **Total cooking
time 30 minutes.**

creamy four-cheese pasta

Serves **4**

Total cooking time **20 minutes**

400 g (13 oz) **dried messicani pasta**

200 g (7 oz) **mascarpone cheese** or **cream cheese**

75 g (3 oz) **mild Gorgonzola cheese**, crumbled

75 g (3 oz) **Fontina cheese**, grated

25 g (1 oz) **Parmesan cheese**, grated

salt and **pepper**

Watercress salad

1 teaspoon **white wine vinegar**

1 tablespoon **extra virgin olive oil**

75 g (3 oz) **watercress**

Cook the pasta in a large saucepan of salted boiling water according to the pack instructions until al dente. Drain, reserving at least 50 ml (2 fl oz) of the cooking water, and return to the pan. Stir in the cheeses, adding enough of the cooking water to make a creamy sauce, and season.

Whisk together the vinegar and oil for the watercress salad, then toss together with the watercress in a bowl and season well.

Spoon the pasta into warmed serving bowls and serve topped with the watercress salad.

For four-cheese tortelloni with yogurt & watercress,

tip 150 g (5 oz) natural yogurt into a heatproof bowl, place over a saucepan of simmering water (making sure the bottom of the bowl doesn't touch the water) and heat through for 5 minutes. Meanwhile, cook 500 g (1 lb) fresh four-cheese tortelloni according to the pack instructions, then drain and return to the pan. Toss through the yogurt and a handful of chopped watercress. Serve immediately. **Total cooking time 10 minutes.**

vegetable, fruit & nut biryani

Serves **4**

Total cooking time **30 minutes**

250 g (8 oz) **basmati rice**

½ **cauliflower**, broken into
florets

2 tablespoons **vegetable oil**

2 large **sweet potatoes**,
peeled and cut into cubes

1 large **onion**, sliced

3 tablespoons **hot curry paste**

½ teaspoon **ground turmeric**

2 teaspoons **mustard seeds**

300 ml (½ pint) hot **vegetable
stock**

250 g (8 oz) **fine green
beans**, halved

100 g (3½ oz) **sultanas**

6 tablespoons chopped **fresh
coriander**

50 g (2 oz) **cashew nuts**,
lightly toasted

Bring a large saucepan of lightly salted water to the
boil and cook the rice for 5 minutes. Add the cauliflower
and cook with the rice for a further 10 minutes or until
both are tender, then drain.

Meanwhile, heat the oil in a large, heavy-based frying
pan and cook the sweet potatoes and onion over a
medium heat, stirring occasionally, for 10 minutes until
browned and tender. Add the curry paste, turmeric and
mustard seeds and cook, stirring, for a further 2 minutes.

Pour in the stock and add the green beans. Bring to the
boil, then reduce the heat and simmer for 5 minutes.

Stir in the drained rice and cauliflower, sultanas,
coriander and cashew nuts and simmer for a further
2 minutes. Serve spooned on to warmed serving plates
with poppadums and raita.

For speedy vegetable biryani, cook 250 g (8 oz)
frozen cauliflower florets and 250 g (8 oz) frozen
green beans in a large saucepan of lightly salted
water according to the pack instructions. Drain and
return to the pan, add a 400 g (13 oz) jar biryani
curry sauce and heat through gently. Meanwhile, heat
400 g (13 oz) ready-cooked pilau rice according to
the pack instructions. Serve the rice alongside the
curry, scattered with lightly toasted cashew nuts, with
poppadums and raita. **Total cooking time 10 minutes.**

baked egg pots with blue cheese

Serves **4**

Total cooking time **20 minutes**

75 g (3 oz) **blue cheese**,
   such as Stilton, Roquefort or
   Gorgonzola, crumbled
150 ml (¼ pint) **double cream**
2 tablespoons chopped
   chives
½ teaspoon **cracked black**
   pepper
butter, for greasing and
   spreading
4 large **eggs**
4 slices of **Granary bread**

Mash the blue cheese into the cream in a small bowl using the back of a fork. Stir in the chives and cracked black pepper then divide the mixture between 4 greased small ramekins.

Crack an egg into each ramekin and place them in a roasting tin. Pour hot water into the tin so that it comes about halfway up the sides of the ramekins. Cook in a preheated oven, 200°C (400°F), Gas Mark 6 for 7−8 minutes, or until the egg whites are set but the yolks are still runny.

Meanwhile, toast the bread until golden and butter lightly. Cut into strips for dipping.

Remove the baked eggs from the oven and serve immediately with the toast.

For creamy scrambled eggs with blue cheese,

beat 8 eggs in a bowl with 75 ml (3 fl oz) full-fat milk and plenty of pepper. Melt 15 g (½ oz)1 tablespoon butter in a large, nonstick saucepan until frothy, then pour in the eggs. Once the eggs begin to set, use a heat-resistant rubber spatula to fold gently over a very low heat for 5−6 minutes until the eggs are creamy and lightly set. Remove from the heat and crumble over 75 g (3 oz) blue cheese and 2 tablespoons chopped chives. Serve the eggs spooned over 4 slices of hot, buttered toast. **Total cooking time 10 minutes.**

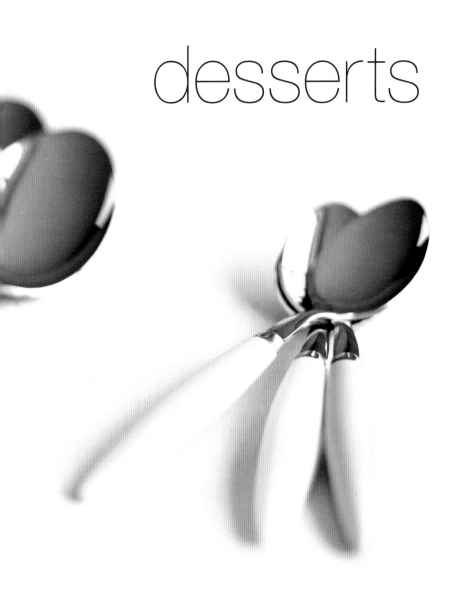

desserts

summer berry charlotte

Serves **4**

Total cooking time **20 minutes**

625 g (1 ¼ lb) **mixed summer
  berries**
1 tablespoon **plain flour**
125 g (4 oz) **caster sugar**
1 teaspoon **vanilla extract**
4–6 slices of **brioche**
softened **butter**, for spreading
vanilla ice cream, to serve

Toss together the berries, flour, sugar and vanilla extract and place in an ovenproof dish.

Cut the brioche slices into triangles, removing the crusts if you like. Butter both sides of the brioche and arrange on top of the berries. Cover the dish with foil and then bake in a preheated oven, 220°C (425°F), Gas Mark 7, for 10 minutes. Uncover and cook for a further 5 minutes until golden and crisp. Serve with vanilla ice cream.

For simple summer pudding, stir together 4 tablespoons blackcurrant cordial, 300 g (10 oz) berry compote and 500 g (1 lb) mixed berries. Leave for a couple of minutes, then drain, reserving the juices in a shallow bowl. Line a 1.2 litre (2 pint) pudding basin with clingfilm. Cut out a circle from a slice of brioche to fit in the bottom of the bowl. Soak the brioche in the fruit juices, then place in the bowl. Cut another 6–8 slices of brioche into long strips, dip into the juices and use to line the sides of the basin, then spoon in the fruit to fill. Cover with some more brioche slices and pour over the remaining juice. Cover with clingfilm, place a small plate on top and weigh down with a heavy can. Leave in the fridge for 10–15 minutes, then turn out on to a serving plate. Serve with cream. **Total cooking time 30 minutes.**

sweet almond frittata

Serves **4**

Total cooking time **30 minutes**

5 large **eggs**

125 g (4 oz) **icing sugar**, plus extra for dusting

75 ml (3 fl oz) **double cream**

50 g (2 oz) **ground almonds**

1 teaspoon **vanilla extract** (optional)

25 g (1 oz) **butter**

50 g (2 oz) **flaked almonds**

vanilla ice cream or **crème fraîche**, to serve

Beat the eggs in a large bowl with 100 g (3½ oz) of the icing sugar, the cream, ground almonds and vanilla extract, if using.

Melt the butter in a large ovenproof frying pan and pour in the egg mixture. Cook very gently for 8–10 minutes, stirring occasionally, until the egg just begins to set. Scatter over the flaked almonds and sprinkle with the remaining icing sugar, then place in a preheated oven 200°C (400°F), Gas Mark 6, for about 10 minutes, until set.

Remove the pan from the oven and place under a preheated medium grill for 2–3 minutes, until golden, then cool slightly and cut into slices. Dust with icing sugar and serve with vanilla ice cream or crème fraîche.

For sweet almond grilled pancakes, beat 50 g (2 oz) ground almonds, 1 teaspoon vanilla extract and all but 2 tablespoons of 125 g (4 oz) icing sugar into 200 g (7 oz) mascarpone cheese. Divide the mixture between 8 small ready-made sweet pancakes, then fold over and arrange in a large ovenproof dish. Scatter with 50 g (2 oz) flaked almonds and sprinkle over the reserved icing sugar. Cook under a preheated grill for 3–4 minutes until warmed and lightly golden. **Total cooking time 10 minutes.**

creamy vanilla rice pudding

Serves **4**

Total cooking time **30 minutes**

125 g (4 oz) **pudding rice**
about 750 ml (1¼ pints) **full
  fat milk**
50 g (2 oz) **caster sugar**
1 **teaspoon vanilla extract**
  or 1 **vanilla pod**, split
25 g (1 oz) **butter**

Place all the ingredients in a saucepan and bring to the boil. Reduce the heat and simmer gently for 25–28 minutes, stirring frequently and adding more milk if necessary, until the rice is creamy and just tender.

Remove the vanilla pod, if using, spoon the rice pudding into bowls and serve immediately.

For crème brûlée rice pudding, spoon 625 g (1¼ lb) chilled ready-made rice pudding into 4 individual ovenproof dishes. Sprinkle the surface generously with 50 g (2 oz) caster sugar, then cook under a preheated hot grill for 3–4 minutes, until the sugar begins to caramelize. Leave to cool for a minute or two so that the sugar hardens, then serve immediately. **Total cooking time 10 minutes.**

banoffee pancakes

Serves **4**

Total cooking time **10 minutes**

4 large or 8 small **ready-made
   sweet pancakes**
6 tablespoons **ready-made
   toffee sauce**, warmed
2 **bananas**, sliced
150 ml (¼ pint) **double** or
   whipping cream
2 tablespoons coarsely grated
   dark chocolate
   or 2 **plain chocolate
   digestive biscuits**, crushed

Place the pancakes on 4 plates and drizzle over the toffee sauce. Scatter the sliced bananas over half of each pancake, then fold over to enclose.

Whip the cream to soft peaks, then place a spoonful on each pancake. Sprinkle with the grated chocolate or crushed chocolate digestive biscuits and serve.

For baked banoffee split, place 4 large bananas on a baking sheet and cook in a preheated oven, 180°C (350°F), Gas Mark 4, for about 12 minutes until blackened and soft. Meanwhile, gently warm 6 tablespoons ready-made toffee sauce or 150 g (5 oz) dulce de leche in a small saucepan, and whip 150 ml (¼ pint) double or whipping cream to soft peaks. Remove the baked bananas from the oven and cut a slit down the centre of each. Arrange in bowls and drizzle the warmed sauce over the bananas. Spoon over the whipped cream, sprinkle with 2 tablespoons coarsely grated plain chocolate and serve. **Total cooking time 20 minutes.**

buttery brioche pudding

Serves **4**

Total cooking time **30 minutes**

50 g (2 oz) **butter**, softened,
   plus extra for greasing
8 thick slices of **brioche**
3 **eggs**, beaten
4 tablespoons **sugar**
450 ml (¾ pint) **full-fat milk**
1 teaspoon **vanilla extract**
   (optional)
75 g (3 oz) **sultanas**
single cream, to serve
   (optional)

Spread butter over both sides of each brioche slice. Heat a nonstick frying pan and fry the brioche slices for 1−2 minutes on each side until crisp and golden.

Whisk together the eggs, sugar, milk and vanilla extract, if using.

Arrange the brioche slices in a greased large ovenproof dish, scatter with sultanas and pour over the egg mixture. Cook in a preheated oven, 180°C (350°F), Gas Mark 4 for 20−25 minutes until just set and lightly golden. Serve with single cream for pouring, if liked.

For buttery brioche with ice cream, spread both sides of 8 thick brioche slices with softened butter, then sprinkle with 4 tablespoons sugar. Heat a nonstick frying pan and fry the brioche slices for 1−2 minutes on each side until crisp and golden. Cut into triangles and arrange on serving plates with scoops of vanilla ice cream, scattered with 75 g (3 oz) sultanas. **Total cooking time 10 minutes.**

soft raspberry meringues

Serves **4**
Total cooking time **30 minutes**

2 **egg whites**
100 g (3½ oz) **caster sugar**
50 g (2 oz) **fresh raspberries**,
   plus extra to serve
crème fraîche, to serve

Line a large baking sheet with nonstick baking parchment. In a clean bowl, whisk the egg whites using a hand-held electric whisk until stiff. Add the sugar, 1 tablespoon at a time, whisking well between each addition, until firm and glossy.

Place the raspberries in a bowl and crush with a fork, then lightly fold through the meringue to form a rippled effect. Place large spoonfuls of the mixture on the prepared baking sheet.

Bake in a preheated oven, 180°C (350°F), Gas Mark 4, for 20 minutes until firm on the outside. Serve with crème fraîche and extra raspberries.

For floating islands with raspberries, in a clean bowl, whisk 2 egg whites using a hand-held electric whisk until stiff. Add 100 g (3½ oz) caster sugar, 1 tablespoon at a time, whisking well between each addition, until firm and glossy. Poach spoonfuls of the meringue in a saucepan of simmering water for 2–3 minutes until firm. Drain with a slotted spoon. Pour a little warmed ready-made custard over the bases of 4 serving bowls, scatter over some fresh raspberries and place the poached meringues on top. **Total cooking time 20 minutes.**

oat-topped orchard fruit crumbles

Serves **4**
Total cooking time **30 minutes**

4 **cooking apples**, peeled,
   cored and roughly chopped
2 tablespoons **soft light
   brown sugar**
2 tablespoons **caster sugar**
3 tablespoons **water**
175 g (6 oz) **blackberries**
100 g (3½ oz) **plain flour**
75 g (3 oz) **unsalted butter**,
   cut into cubes
100 g (3½ oz) **porridge oats**
100 g (3½ oz) **demerara
   sugar**
½ teaspoon **ground
   cinnamon**
clotted cream, ice cream or
   crème fraîche, to serve

Place the apples, brown sugar, caster sugar and measurement water in a heavy-based saucepan and cook over a gentle heat, stirring occasionally, for 5–8 minutes until the apples are soft and just beginning to turn pulpy. Fold in the blackberries, cover and remove from the heat. Keep warm.

Sift the flour into a large bowl, add the butter and rub in with the fingertips until the mixture resembles coarse breadcrumbs. Stir in the oats, demerara sugar and cinnamon. Spread the crumble mixture out in a large roasting tin and place in a preheated oven, 200°C (400°F), Gas Mark 6, for 10–15 minutes, stirring halfway through cooking, until golden.

Spoon the warm fruit into warmed serving bowls and top with the warm golden crumble. Serve with clotted cream, ice cream or crème fraîche.

For mixed summer fruit crumbles, divide 200 g (7 oz) frozen mixed summer fruits between 4 small ramekins. Sprinkle 2 teaspoons vanilla sugar and 1 teaspoon cornflour over each ramekin and stir around a little. Cover each with 1–2 tablespoons ready-made crumble mix. Stand the ramekins on a baking sheet and place in a preheated oven, 220°C (425°F), Gas Mark 7, for 15 minutes. Serve with vanilla ice cream. **Total cooking time 20 minutes.**

syrup sponge microwave puds

Serves **4**

Total cooking time **20 minutes**

100 g (3½ oz) **butter**, softened, plus extra for greasing
100 g (3½ oz) **soft light brown sugar**
100 g (3½ oz) **self-raising flour**
1 teaspoon **mixed spice**
1 **egg**, beaten
4 tablespoons **golden syrup**
ready-made custard, to serve

Grease 4 x 150 ml (¼ pint) ramekins lightly and line the bases with nonstick baking parchment. Beat the butter with the sugar in a bowl until pale and fluffy, then sift in the flour and spice and add the beaten egg. Beat together until well mixed.

Divide the mixture between the prepared ramekins. Cover each with a disc of nonstick baking parchment and cook together in a microwave oven on high for 2–2½ minutes, then leave the sponges to rest for 3–4 minutes to finish cooking.

Turn each pudding out on to a serving plate and drizzle each with 1 tablespoon of the golden syrup while still warm. Serve with custard.

For baked treacle sponge, grease a 1 litre (1¾ pint) shallow baking dish and spoon in 6 tablespoons golden syrup. In a food processor, whizz together 100 g (3½ oz) each softened butter and caster sugar, 2 beaten eggs and 1 teaspoon vanilla extract. Add 100 g (3½ oz) self-raising flour and pulse until just mixed. Scrape into the baking dish and place in a preheated oven, 180°C (350°F), Gas Mark 4, for 25 minutes until golden. Serve with hot shop-bought ready-made custard. **Total cooking time 30 minutes.**

apple & oaty crunch

Serves **4**

Total cooking time **20 minutes**

25 g (1 oz) **unsalted butter**

2 large **Bramley cooking apples**, peeled, cored and cut into chunks

4 tablespoons **soft dark brown sugar**

4 tablespoons **double cream**

8 tablespoons **granola crunchy oat cereal**

2 tablespoons **toasted flaked almonds**

clotted cream, to serve (optional)

Melt the butter in a heavy-based frying pan and cook the apple chunks over a medium heat, stirring occasionally, for 5–6 minutes until tender and browned.

Add the sugar and cook, stirring, for 1 minute. Add the cream and cook, stirring, for a further 1 minute until the sauce is caramel coloured and the apples are tender yet still retaining their shape.

Divide the apple mixture between 4 warmed serving bowls. Mix the oat cereal with the almonds and spoon over the top of the hot apple mixture. Serve with a spoonful of clotted cream on top, if liked.

For apple & raspberry grilled crumbles, mix a 400 g (13 oz) can or jar prepared apples or apple pie filling with 100 g (3½ oz) fresh raspberries and divide between 4 individual ramekins. Top with 8 tablespoons granola crunchy cereal mixed with 2 tablespoons ground almonds. Dot with butter and cook under a preheated medium grill for 2 minutes until warm. Serve with vanilla ice cream. **Total cooking time 10 minutes.**

chocolate puddle pudding

Serves **4**

Total cooking time **30 minutes**

75 g (3 oz) **unsalted butter**, softened

75 g (3 oz) **soft light brown sugar**

3 **eggs**

65 g (2½ oz) **self-raising flour**

3 tablespoons **cocoa powder**

½ teaspoon **baking powder**

icing sugar, for dusting

ice cream or **cream**, to serve

Sauce

2 tablespoons **cocoa powder**

50 g (2 oz) **soft light brown sugar**

250 ml (8 fl oz) boiling **water**

Grease a 600 ml (1 pint) gratin dish with a little of the butter. Place the remaining butter, brown sugar and eggs in a large bowl and sift in the flour, cocoa and baking powder. Beat together until smooth. Spoon the mixture into the prepared dish and spread the top level.

Place the cocoa and sugar in a bowl for the sauce and mix in a little of the measurement water to make a smooth paste, then add the remaining water, a little at a time, and mix until smooth.

Pour the sauce over the pudding mixture and place in a preheated oven, 200°C (400°F), Gas Mark 6, for 15 minutes or until the sauce has sunk to the bottom of the dish and the pudding is well risen. Dust with icing sugar and serve with ice cream or cream.

For chocolate sponges with hot chocolate sauce, heat 4 ready-made chocolate sponge cakes or muffins in a microwave oven for 1 minute until warmed through. Meanwhile, mix 1 teaspoon finely grated orange rind into 100 g (3½ oz) clotted cream. Make the chocolate sauce as above. Serve the warm cakes or muffins covered with the hot sauce and topped with a spoonful of the orange cream. **Total cooking time 10 minutes.**

tropical fruit cheesecakes

Serves **2**

Total cooking time **30 minutes**

25 g (1 oz) **butter**

75 g (3 oz) **coconut biscuits**, crushed

125 g (4 oz) **full-fat soft cheese**

3 tablespoons **condensed milk**

finely grated rind and juice of 1 **lime**

2 tablespoons diced **pineapple** and **mango flesh**

Melt the butter in a small saucepan and stir in the crushed biscuits. Divide between 2 dessert glasses and press down with the back of a spoon.

Mix together the soft cheese, condensed milk, most of the lime rind (reserving a little for decoration) and the lime juice in a bowl. Spoon over the biscuit bases and spread evenly. Cover and chill in the refrigerator for 10 minutes.

Top with the pineapple and mango, decorate with the reserved lime rind and serve.

For tropical fruit salad with coconut cream, place 250 g (8 oz) ready-prepared tropical fruits, ½ piece of stem ginger, sliced, and 2 tablespoons stem ginger syrup from the jar in a bowl and stir well to coat the fruit in the syrup. Mix together 4 tablespoons crème fraîche, a pinch of ground ginger and 1 teaspoon desiccated coconut in a separate bowl, mix well and serve with the fruit salad. **Total cooking time 10 minutes.**

quick tiramisu with strawberries

Serves **4–6**

Total cooking time **30 minutes**

150 ml (¼ pint) **strong coffee**, cooled

75 g (3 oz) **soft light brown sugar**

4 tablespoons **coffee liqueur**

100 g (3½ oz) **sponge fingers**, snapped in half

300 ml (½ pint) **ready-made fresh custard**

250 g (8 oz) **mascarpone cheese**

1 teaspoon **vanilla extract**

125 g (4 oz) **plain dark chocolate**, roughly chopped

125 g (4 oz) **fresh strawberries**, hulled and thinly sliced

cocoa powder, for dusting

Place the coffee, sugar and liqueur in a large bowl. Add the sponge fingers and gently toss to soak in the mixture, then transfer to a shallow serving dish, spooning over any excess liquid.

Beat the custard with the mascarpone and vanilla extract in a separate bowl, then spoon half over the soaked biscuits and spread evenly. Scatter half the chocolate over the top followed by the strawberries.

Spoon the remaining mascarpone mixture over the strawberries and spread evenly. Scatter over the remaining chocolate and dust with cocoa. Cover and chill for 15 minutes or until ready to serve.

For Irish cream liqueur tiramisu, press 8 halved sponge fingers into 4 glass serving dishes. Pour over enough cold coffee to soak the sponges. Sprinkle 1 tablespoon Irish cream liqueur over each dish, then top each with 1 scoop Irish cream liqueur ice cream, 1 tablespoon softly whipped cream and a sprinkling of grated plain dark chocolate. Serve immediately. Total cooking time 10 minutes.

rhubarb fool

Serves **4**

Total cooking time **30 minutes**

450 g (14½ oz) **rhubarb**, chopped into bite-sized pieces

2 tablespoons **caster sugar**

4 tablespoons **white wine**

300 ml (½ pint) **double cream**

finely grated rind of **1 lemon**

1 egg white

chopped **pistachio nuts**, to serve

Place the rhubarb and sugar in a saucepan over a low heat, pour in the wine and simmer until cooked. Pour into a bowl and leave to cool.

Whisk the cream until thick and stir into the rhubarb with the grated lemon rind.

Whisk the egg white in a clean bowl until stiff, then gently fold into the rhubarb mixture.

Divide between 4 bowls and top with the chopped pistachios. Cover and chill until required.

For roasted rhubarb, cut 550 g (1 lb 2 oz) rhubarb into finger-sized pieces. Place in a shallow ovenproof dish and toss with 85 g (3¼ oz) caster sugar, making sure the rhubarb is in a single layer. Cover with foil and roast in a preheated oven, 200°C (400°F), Gas Mark 6, for 15 minutes. Remove the foil and continue to cook for a further 5–6 minutes until the rhubarb is tender and the juices are syrupy. Serve with vanilla ice cream. **Total cooking time 30 minutes.**

baked apples with spiced fruit

Serves **4**
Total cooking time **30 minutes**

4 **cooking apples**, cored and
    scored around the middle
75 g (3 oz) **dried cranberries**
4 pieces of **stem ginger**,
    diced
finely grated rind of 2 **oranges**
½ teaspoon **mixed spice**
4 tablespoons **clear honey**
2 tablespoons **water**
crème fraîche, to serve

Place the apples in an ovenproof dish. Mix together the cranberries, stem ginger, orange rind, mixed spice and honey, then spoon the mixture into the cavity of each apple.

Pour the measurement water into the dish. Bake in a preheated oven, 190°C (375°F), Gas Mark 5, for 22–25 minutes until the apples are puffy and cooked through. Serve with crème fraîche.

For spiced apples, melt 25 g (1 oz) butter in a frying pan over a medium heat, add 4 peeled, cored and sliced apples and ½ tablespoon mixed spice and cook for 5–6 minutes. Stir in 2 tablespoons clear honey. Serve with crème fraîche. **Total cooking time 10 minutes.**

lemon & passionfruit whips

Serves **2**
Total cooking time **10 minutes**

50 g (2 oz) **shortbread
  biscuits**, crushed
150 ml (¼ pint) **double cream**
120 g (4 oz) pot **lemon yogurt**
2 **passionfruit**, halved

Divide the crushed biscuits between 2 glasses. Whip the cream in a bowl until just thick enough to form soft peaks, then lightly fold in the yogurt with the seeds and pulp from 1 of the passionfruit.

Spoon the mixture into the glasses and spoon the remaining passionfruit seeds and pulp over the top.

For lemon & passionfruit syllabubs, divide the seeds and pulp from 1 halved passionfruit between 2 glasses. Using a hand-held electric whisk, whisk together 150 ml (¼ pint) double cream, 3 tablespoons medium-dry white wine, 40 g (1½ oz) caster sugar, the finely grated rind of ½ lemon and the seeds and pulp from 1 halved passionfruit in a bowl until the mixture is thick enough to form soft peaks when the whisk is lifted. Spoon into the glasses, cover and chill for 5–10 minutes. Serve with shortbread biscuits. **Total cooking time 20 minutes.**

warm apricots with mascarpone

Serves **4**

Total cooking time **20 minutes**

25 g (1 oz) **butter**

375 g (12 oz) **apricots**, stoned and quartered

50 g (2 oz) **soft light brown sugar**

6 tablespoons **stem ginger syrup**

2 pieces of **stem ginger**, finely chopped

250 g (8 oz) tub **mascarpone cheese**

2 tablespoons **demerara sugar**

toasted slices of **brioche**, to serve

Melt the butter in a heavy-based frying pan and cook the apricots over a medium heat, stirring occasionally, for 3–4 minutes until soft and browned in places. Sprinkle over the brown sugar and cook, stirring, for 1 minute. Add the stem ginger syrup, stir well and cook for a further 1 minute, then remove from the heat.

Mix the chopped stem ginger with the mascarpone and demerara sugar.

Serve the apricots on warm toasted brioche with a spoonful of the ginger cream on top, allowing it to melt.

For quick gingered apricots with amaretti, melt 25 g (1 oz) butter in a heavy-based saucepan and cook a well-drained 400 g (13 oz) can halved apricots over a high heat, stirring, for 2–3 minutes. Sprinkle over 50 g (2 oz) soft light brown sugar and cook for 2–3 minutes, allowing the sugar to caramelize slightly. Pour over 2 tablespoons orange juice and heat for 1 minute, then transfer to a warmed serving dish and scatter over 8 lightly crushed amaretti biscuits. Serve with Greek yogurt. **Total cooking time 10 minutes.**

pan-fried toffee apples

Serves **4**

Total cooking time **20 minutes**

75 g (3 oz) **butter**
4 **dessert apples**, cored and
   cut into wedges
75 g (3 oz) **soft light brown
   sugar**
75 ml (3 fl oz) **double cream**

Heat the butter in a large frying pan, add the apple wedges and fry for 5 minutes until soft and golden. Remove from the pan and set aside.

Add the sugar to the butter and juices in the pan and heat gently, stirring to dissolve the sugar. Simmer for 1 minute, then stir in the cream and heat through for 1 minute.

Return the apples to the pan and coat in the toffee sauce. Cool slightly, then serve.

For toffee apple pecan waffles, heat 25 g (1 oz) butter in a large frying pan, add 4 peeled and cored dessert apples, cut into wedges, and fry over a gentle heat for 3–4 minutes until soft and golden. Stir in 8 tablespoons ready-made toffee sauce, such as dulce de leche, and a few pecan nut halves and heat through for 1 minute. Serve on toasted waffles. **Total cooking time 10 minutes.**

caramelized custard tarts

Serves **4**

Total cooking time **30 minutes**

375 g (12 oz) **ready-rolled puff pastry**
pinch of **ground nutmeg**
½ teaspoon **ground cinnamon**
2 tablespoons **caster sugar**
plain flour, for dusting

Filling
3 **egg yolks**
50 g (2 oz) **caster sugar**
2 tablespoons **cornflour**
1 teaspoon **vanilla extract**
finely grated rind of ¼ **lemon**
300 ml (½ pint) **double cream**

Unwrap the pastry and sprinkle over the nutmeg, cinnamon and caster sugar. Then tightly roll up the pastry, like a Swiss roll, and cut it into 12 x 1.5 cm (¾ inch) slices (you may have some pastry left over). Roll each slice into a small round on a lightly floured surface. Turn a 12-hole muffin tin upside down, gently press each round over the top of a muffin mould and chill in the freezer for 5 minutes.

Bake in a preheated oven, 220°C (425°F), Gas Mark 7, for 5 minutes, then remove the pastry cases from the muffin tin and place on a baking sheet.

Meanwhile, for the filling, put the egg yolks, the caster sugar, cornflour, vanilla extract and lemon rind in a bowl and whisk until smooth. Add the cream and whisk again, then cook in a saucepan for 5 minutes, stirring frequently, until the mixture is thick, taking care not to let it boil.

Spoon the custard into the pastry cases. Turn up the oven to 230°C (450°F), Gas Mark 8, and bake for 12–15 minutes until caramelized and set.

For creamy caramel, whip 300 ml (½ pint) double cream until soft peaks form, then stir in 3 tablespoons ready-made caramel sauce. Spoon into 4 serving bowls. Sprinkle over a little ground cinnamon and drizzle with some more caramel sauce. Serve with tuile biscuits. **Total cooking time 10 minutes.**

index

acknowledgements

Commissioning editor: Eleanor Maxfield
Editor: Sybella Stephens
Designer: Tracy Killick
Production controller: Sarah Kramer

Photography: Stephen Conroy 2, 17, 25, 37, 67, 71, 73, 75, 79, 81, 105, 121, 129, 173, 187, 193, 211, 213, 215, 217, 221, 229; Will Heap 1, 6, 7, 8, 15, 29, 31, 33, 35, 63, 69, 77, 117, 125, 155, 157, 159, 175, 177, 199, 233; David Munns 54, 100; Lis Parsons 10, 13, 19, 21, 23, 27, 39, 41, 43, 45, 47, 49, 51, 53, 57, 59, 61, 85, 87, 95, 99, 113, 123, 127, 137, 161, 163, 165, 167, 179, 185, 189, 196, 209, 219, 227, 231; William Reavell 4, 9, 65, 89, 91, 97, 143, 151, 171, 181, 195, 201, 203, 205, 207; Craig Robertson 83, 169, 183, 191; William Shaw 93, 103, 107, 109, 111, 115, 119, 139, 141, 145, 147, 149, 152, 223, 225.